The Ca B%K Of Statistics

Taking the Carry Ons into a new century

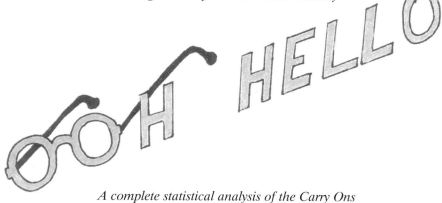

A complete statistical analysis of the Carry Ons

by

Kevin Snelgrove

Foreword by Alan Hume
Introduction by Jack Douglas

Published by KAS Publications, Frome, Somerset
First Edition printed April 2003

ISBN 0-9544200-0-4

Front and back covers designed by Pete Dayman-Johns
Picture from *Carry On Teacher*
© Canal + Image UK Ltd 1959

Typeset by TW Typesetting, Midsomer Norton, Somerset
Printed in Great Britain by Antony Rowe Ltd, Chippenham, Wiltshire

In Memory
Of
Paul Antony Snelgrove
24.4.1962 – 20.1.2000

Contents

They gave so much laughter to millions of people and still continue to do so....

The entrance to Pinewood studios, the home of the Carry Ons

Acknowledgements

I would like to thank all of the people who stood by me from the start while producing the book and with putting up with the constant Carry On stories from the great days had at Pinewood Carry On Conventions and Events.

For their support and contributions a very special thank you to the following...
Terence Alexander, Malcom Allen, Robin Askwith, Lynda Baron, Morris Bright, Graham C Bromwich, Sheila Boundford, Jim Brownlie, Peter Byrne, Gerald Campion, David Claydon, Alexandra Dane, Ed Devereaux, Jack Douglas, Patrick Durkin, Shirley Eaton, Heather Emmanuel, Hilda Fenemore, Fenella Fielding, Liz Fraser, Hugh Futcher, Peter Gilmore, Jennifer Govey, Mike Grady, Melvyn Hayes, Sally-Victoria Higgs, Julian Hill, Norman Hudis, Alan Hume, Laraine Humphreys, Oscar James, Sue James, Valerie James, Pete Dayman-Johns, Vivienne Johnson, Anna Karen, Rosiland Knight, Burt Kwouk, Marjie Lawerence, Dilys Laye, Valerie Leon, Natalie May, Don McCorkindale, Desmond McNamara, Janet Moat, Richard O'Callaghan, Milo O'Shea, Christine Ozanne, Nicholas Parsons, Bill Pertwee, Nosher Powell, Linda Regan, Anton Rodgers, Peter Rogers, Robert Ross, Ann Runeckles, Valerie Shute, Sir Donald Sinden C.B.E, Marc Sinden, Audrey Skinner, Ronnie Stevens, Marianne Stone, Philip Stone, Christina Sutch, Frank Thornton, Harry Towb, Wanda Ventham, Valerie Van Ost, and June Whitfield C.B.E.

An extra special thank you to Peter Rogers for the use of the Carry On name.

John Heron of Canal+ Image UK Ltd Pinewood Studios.

Extract from *Confessions of Robin Askwith* by Robin Askwith. Published by Ebury. Used by permission of The Random House Group Limited.

To Mum and Terry for the loan of the car. To Andrew for carrying on!

Also to my wife Julie who suffered from Carry Onitis –
until she began to really enjoy them.

And finally to Samantha, Kate, Charlotte and Samuel
the new breed of Carry On fan.

Foreword
by Alan Hume

It is a great pleasure to have been asked to write the foreword for your new book, *The Carry On B%k of Statistics*.

Carry On and on and on for thirty productions, the most prolific series of feature film comedies from England or any other country. Not everybody's taste, but over 60% of filmgoers in the UK and other parts of the world loved them.

The producer Peter Rogers masterminded every script, also the casting of the artists who were wonderfully talented actors.

Peter's director Gerald Thomas was an expert director and very talented film editor. His expertise got the utmost out of each script, his editing and direction giving the actors every opportunity to get as much fun and laughter over to the audience as possible.

Peter Rogers and Gerald Thomas were a very strong team, none of these thirty Carry On films were ever over schedule or over budget, a unique achievement in the unpredictable business of film production.

I was lucky enough to work as a cameraman on sixteen Carry On films, every day was a pleasure to be there, and the happiest, funniest film set I ever worked on. Often there would be hilarious laughter behind the camera at the antics going on in front of the camera.

One such I found not quite so amusing was when I allowed Charles Hawtrey to ride my Lambretta around the car park for a shot in *Carry On Cabby* (1963). Charles was no rider or driver and in trying to negotiate the way around parked cars he managed to run my Lambretta into my parked car, denting both in one go. Fortunately he was unscathed. So once again a Carry On was completed on schedule and on budget.

Enjoy these interesting statistics from the famous Carry Ons...

Introduction
by Jack Douglas

Dear Reader,

What do I know about statistics? (other than 38-24-36 – Tee Hee)

Ah, just thought of one. Out of the thirty-one *Carry On* pictures – by the way I did the last eight – believe it or not they were all made in the record time of six weeks. We all enjoyed them so much it was like playtime at school!

Even though most of the team are now gone, they will live on forever on the screen.

So Carry On Reading

Hope you enjoy the book

About the Carry Ons

For over forty-five years the Carry Ons have been a part of the British way of life. The picture-postcard humour was brought to life way back in 1958 with *Carry On Sergeant*, a film scripted by Norman Hudis, produced by Peter Rogers and directed by Gerald Thomas. After the success of *Sergeant*, *Carry On Nurse* followed, which was to be a number one box office hit in 1959 and is a cult film today on the campus's in the USA. Hudis went on to write another four films, *Teacher* (1959), *Constable* (1959), *Regardless* (1960) and *Cruising* (1962). In 1963 a new script writer came on to the scene by the name of Talbot Rothwell, who started with *Cabby* (1963), and went on to write another nineteen films in the series, finishing with *Dick* in 1974. The Rogers and Thomas partnership averaged almost two films per year until the end of 1971. In this year *At Your Convenience* was released. It took almost five years for this film to make its money back. The Carry On films were starting to take a downward slide which was resurrected in 1974 with *Dick* and almost peaked before it's fall in 1976 with *England* and then finally in 1992 with *Columbus,* yet this film did make its money quickly. The Carry On films were finished for now! Yet Peter Rogers has said at a Carry On Convention "that if a good enough script was written he would consider making another one", so they may not be finished.

In between the films a television programme was produced in 1969, *Carry On Christmas*. Another nineteen followed until the last programme in 1989, *Norbert Smith – A Life*. Though these were good they were never as popular as the films.

In 1973 *Carry On London*, the first of three stage shows, was performed at the Victoria Palace. This ran for a year and a half and starred many of the Carry On team that appeared in the films. The final stage show was *Wot a Carry On* in Blackpool and ran for five months, though most of the team had now departed from this world to appear in the great Carry On in the sky. So the Carry Ons ended in 1992 with both the last film and the last stage show.

So Carry On gaining knowledge!

The home of the Carry Ons Pinewood Studios

CARRY ON SERGEANT
SCENE 1   TAKE 1

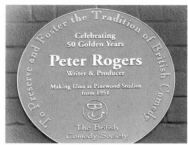

Chapter 1
The Films

A–Z Guide

A is for *Abroad* (1972), *Again Doctor* (1969), *At Your Convenience* (1971),
           Again Christmas (1970) and *And in my Lady's Chamber* (1975)   = 5
B is for *Behind* (1975)   = 1
C is for *Cabby* (1963), *Camping* (1968), *Cleo* (1964), *Columbus* (1992),
           Constable (1959), *Cowboy* (1965), *Cruising* (1962), *Christmas (1969),
           Christmas* (1972), *Christmas* (1973) and *Christmas Classics* (1983) = 11
D is for *Dick* (1974), *Doctor* (1967) and *Don't Lose Your Head* (1966)   = 3
E is for *Emmannuelle* (1978) and *England* (1976)   = 2
F is for *Follow that Camel* (1967)   = 1
G is for *Girls* (1973)   = 1
H is for *Henry* (1970)   = 1
J is for *Jack* (1963)   = 1
L is for *Loving* (1970), *Lamp-Posts of the Empire* (1975), *London* (1973/5)
           and *Laughing with The Slimming Factory* (1975)   = 4
M is for *Matron* (1971)   = 1
N is for *Nurse* (1958) and *Norbert Smith – A Life* (1989)   = 2
O is for *Orgy & Bess* (1975) and *One in the Eye for Harold* (1975)   = 2
R is for *Regardless* (1960)   = 1
S is for *Sergeant* (1958), *Screaming* (1966), *Spying* (1964)
           and *Short Knights, Long Daze* (1975)   = 4
T is for *Teacher* (1959), *That's Carry On* (1977), *The Prisoner of
           Spenda* (1975), *The Baron Outlook* (1975), *The Sobbing
           Cavalier* (1975), *The Nine Old Cobblers* (1975), *The Case
           of the Screaming Winkles* (1975) and *The Case of the Coughing
           Parrot* (1975)   = 8
U is for *Up The Jungle* (1969), *Up The Khyber* (1968) and *Under the
           Round Table* (1975)   = 3
W is for *What a Carry On* (1973), *Who Needs Kitchener?* (1975) and
           Wot a Carry On in Blackpool (1992)   = 3

CARRY ON MEMORY

"Carry On Columbus was my one and only Carry On film. It wound up
being my shortest performance ever in anything, but at least I was part of
an British institution."

Lynda Baron

Did you know the following?

The following four pages of bullet pointed statistical information are facts from the Carry On's, so read on, it gets far more interesting from here on in...

➢ Production on the Carry On films started on 24th March 1958 with *Sergeant*.

➢ It would cost £984,200 to make a Carry On film at todays' prices – still very cheap.

➢ Most of the Carry On films were filmed on location within a 15 to 20 mile radius of Pinewood Studios.

➢ 2,000,000 plastic daffodils were imported from Japan, they were used to advertise *Nurse* released in 1959.

➢ The wardrobe bill for *Carry On Nurse* was £475.

➢ For his role in *Carry On Sergeant* (1958), Kenneth Williams was paid £800.

➢ For his role in *Cruising* (1962), Kenneth Williams' pay rose to £5,000 per film; Sid James was the only other team member to earn the same.

➢ If only four of the films failed, the pass rate would be an astonishing 87.1% – an excellent achievement in anyone's eyes.

➢ Phil Silvers and Elke Sommer were paid £30,000 each for their roles in *Follow That Camel* (1967) and *Behind* (1975). This was the highest paid in a Carry On.

➢ *Carry On At your Convenience* (1971) took over five years to get its money back.

➢ There was a six-week filming schedule for each Carry On film.

➢ Over eight million viewers watched *Carry On Christmas* in 1969.

➢ *Carry On Emmannuelle* (1978) was the only film to use two studios, of course Pinewood, the other being Wembley.

➢ Norman Hudis wrote the first six Carry On films, *Carry On Regardless* (1960) was the least favourite of the films he had written.

➢ Talbot Rothwell took over as scriptwriter in 1963 and went on to write twenty Carry On films.

➢ Two films, *Carry On Don't Lose Your Head* (1966) and *Carry On Follow that Camel* (1967) were released without the Carry On prefix. Later they added the Carry On name and as a result they were an instant success.

➢ On only one occasion did the team venture out of England to shoot a Carry On film and that was to Snowdonia, North Wales for *Carry On Up The Khyber* in 1968.

➢ In 1959 *Carry On Nurse* was first in the box office ratings, it remains a cult film in the USA to this day.

➢ Bernard Bresslaw's phrase "I Only Arsked" was written into all of the fourteen films he appeared in.

➢ Charles Hawtrey's first line was usually "Ohh Hello".

➢ The first Carry On film to be filmed in colour was *Carry On Cruising* in 1962.

➢ To date there have been fifty-five continuity errors or mistakes made in eighteen of the films, spotted by eagle-eyed Carry On fans.

➢ Eight Carry On films were never made – *What a Carry On* (1961), *Smoking* (1961), *Flying* (1962), *Spaceman* (1962), *Again Nurse* (1979), *Dallas* (1987), *Down Under* (1988) and *Nursing* (1988).

➢ To film a Carry On, they only used one camera, a Mitchell 35mm. They very rarely used two.

➢ When released in the USA, *Carry On Nurse* ran for over two and a half years in Los Angeles, California.

➢ Car Park Number One at Pinewood was used for the taxi yard in *Carry On Cabby* (1963).

➢ The *Carry On Laughing* compilation television series took over nine months to put together. Gerald Thomas used to view miles and miles of film before editing.

> A £500,000 budget was set aside for *Carry On Down Under* in 1988. Gerald Thomas went to Australia to view possible locations but the film was never made. In one way that was good, it kept the films totally British.

> All of the main Carry On actors were offered a percentage of the box office takings by Peter Rogers, but they all turned it down and stuck with their one-off payment per film, a big mistake. Only Kenneth Williams admitted this. The offer was made in the early sixties.

> *Carry On Again Nurse* film script written by Norman Hudis had 148 scenes, it was to be the 30th anniversary film, but it was never made.

> *Carry On Sergeant* (1958) made its money back within two weeks of opening in London.

> The first draft script for *Carry On Sergeant* had a total of 180 pages.

> On the success of the first six Carry On films, *Carry On Admiral* by Val Guest was re-released. It only took £11,000 at the box office nationwide, so the people knew what a real Carry On was.

> Every seven years the Carry On films gains a new audience of fans.

> Not one foot of Carry On film was cut nor edited without the permission of producer Peter Rogers.

> Jack Douglas was given twelve bottles of champagne from Peter Rogers and Gerald Thomas to welcome him to the Carry On team in 1971.

> The warehouse scene in *Carry On Spying* (1964) was shot at 3 am; probably the earliest start on any film, 8 am was the norm.

> Filming usually was Monday to Friday on the Carry On films.

> The Carry On television Christmas specials – Barbara Windsor was the only Carry On regular to appear in all four.

> 96 different locations were used in the making of the Carry On films.

> The longest time spent away on location was three weeks to Camber Sands, Rye, Sussex to film *Carry On Follow That Camel* in 1967.

- Talbot Rothwell took just two weeks to write the script for *Carry On Cabby* (1963).

- In the mid '90s, two Carry On films were put into the top ten films ever made in Britain – they were *Carry On Cleo* (1964) and *Carry On Up The Khyber* (1968). Both ranked in at equal number ten.

- It took three days to film the dinner party scene at the end of *Carry On Up The Khyber* (1968).

- When Jacki Piper started filming her first film *Carry On Up The Jungle* (1969), she was offered a contract for the next two years. She went on to appear in four films.

- Jim Dale suggested that he did his own stunts in the Carry On films. Gerald Thomas always use to leave the stunts for the end of filming. Jim actually broke a bone in his arm when he did the stunts in *Carry On Again Doctor* in (1969).

- Leslie Phillips got credited for his role in *Carry On Regardless* in 1960 – but the thing was he was never in the film. The credit appeared in a Bristol Newspaper.

- The first three Carry On films had a budget of between £70,000 and £80,000.

- In *Carry On Cowboy* (1965) Bernard Bresslaw had to climb fifty feet up into a tree for the shooting scenes.

- *Carry On Sergeant* (1958) was third in the box office ratings.

- Only six of the Carry On films were released on audio cassette. They were *Don't Lose Your Head* (1966), *Follow That Camel* (1967), *Doctor* (1967), *Up The Khyber* (1968), *Camping* (1969) and *Up The Jungle* (1969).

- One of the production crew used a .22 rifle to shoot the bottle out of Sid James' hand in the "dinner party scene" in *Carry On Up The Khyber* (1968).

- It was Kenneth Williams who recommended Jim Dale to join the Carry On team. An excellent recommendation as Jim fitted in really well.

- Talbot Rothwell was paid £4,000 for his script of *Carry On Cleo* in 1964.

- Four policemen were used to protect Robin Askwith and Margaret Nolan's scene together on Brighton beach.

➢ Two policemen and one night watchman were used to guard the fort at Camber Sands.

➢ The Carry On films finished filming on the 27th May 1992 with *Carry On Columbus*.

The South Gates at Pinewood Studios. Scene used in Carry On Screaming *(1966)*

The Hall of Fame entering into the Archive Department at Pinewood Studios. It was used as the opening scene in Carry On Spying *(1964)*

The shops used as the butchers in Carry On Behind *(1975). They are situated in Farnham Common Buckinghamshire*

Carry On Film Statistics

<table>
<tr><td>Totals</td><td>Averages</td></tr>
<tr><td>31 films were made between 1958 and 1992</td><td>1.48 films per year, over a 21-year period, allowing for the break between 1978 and 1992</td></tr>
<tr><td>Around six and a half million was budgeted for the making of all 31 films</td><td>£230,000 to produce each film (approx)</td></tr>
<tr><td>It took 1,303 days = 184.14 weeks = 3.58 years to make all of the films</td><td>It took six weeks to produce a film</td></tr>
<tr><td>Approximately 569.5 miles were travelled on location (as the crow flies)</td><td>18.3 miles traveled for each film on location</td></tr>
<tr><td>Around 1,156 stars and co-stars appeared in the credits to all 31 films</td><td>37 stars and co-stars per film</td></tr>
<tr><td>2,771 minutes of film running time</td><td>89 minutes 39 seconds per film</td></tr>
<tr><td>250,336 feet of film was used</td><td>8,075 feet per film</td></tr>
<tr><td>Some 300 reels of film was used</td><td>10 reels per film</td></tr>
</table>

Filmed in colour	23	74%
Filmed in B/W	7	23%
Filmed in colour & B/W	1	3%
Cert A's	22	71%
Cert U's	7	23%
Cert AA	1	3%
Cert PG	1	3%

Seasons of Fun

A common favourite to most, including the Carry On producer Peter Rogers, was, and still is, *Carry On Up The Khyber* (1968).

This is one of the seven films which started its production in April. In fact almost a quarter of the thirty-one films produced also saw April as their starting time, the reason obviously being the new financial year which brought windfalls of money and of course laughter. The month of March also equalled April with the start of seven productions, the reason probably being that there must have been some money left in the pot. No films started production in the months of June, August and December, this being due to Summer Shows and Christmas Pantomimes. Of course this resulted in most of the ever-popular Carry On team being "inn it again", as Sid said.

The very first film produced *Carry On Sergeant* (1958) finished its filming in May, another nine films followed suit, so a third of the Carry On film series finished their filming within this month.

It took an average of four months for a Carry On film to be released, autumn and winter saw the most films released, nineteen of the amazing thirty-one Carry On films (61.3%), brought us, the public, so much cheer and warmed our cockles on these cold long days.

"Cor!"

CARRY ON MEMORY

"My Carry On memory is *Carry On Abroad* when I was in bed waiting for Ken Connor to leap on top of me knowing that we and the bed were about to crash through the floor below. Luckily it worked the first time but it was a somewhat nervous moment for Ken and me."

June Whitfield CBE

Carry On Films
Month Production Started

1. **March**	7	22.6%
(*Sergeant, Teacher, Cabby, Again Doctor,*		
At Your Convenience, Dick, Behind)		
April	7	22.6%
(*Up The Khyber, Loving, Abroad, Girls,*		
That's Carry On, Emmannuelle, Columbus)		
2. **October** (*Camping, Up The Jungle, Henry, Matron*)	4	12.9%
3. **September** (*Jack, Don't Lose Your Head, Doctor*)	3	9.6%
November (*Nurse, Constable, Regardless*)	3	9.6%
4. **January** (*Cruising, Screaming*)	2	6.5%
May (*Follow That Camel, England*)	2	6.5%
July (*Cleo, Cowboy*)	2	6.5%
5. **February** (*Spying*)	1	3.2%
6. **June, August, December**	0	0%

Spring	16	51.6%
Summer	2	6.5%
Autumn	10	32.3%
Winter	3	9.6%

CARRY ON MEMORY

"Appearing in a Carry On film was like working for a family. Peter Rogers and Gerald Thomas had assembled a group of highly talented comedy performers, who starred regularly in these films. They all knew one another, understood each other's timing, and a great camaraderie existed between them. They worked at speed to get everything filmed on time and within very strict budget limits. A newcomer took a little time to adjust, but it was an enjoyable experience being in one of these films."

Nicholas Parsons

Carry On Films
Month Production Finished

1.	**May**	10	32.2%
	(*Sergeant, Cabby, Up The Khyber, Again Doctor, Loving, At Your Convenience, Abroad, Girls, Emmannuelle, Columbus*)		
2.	**April**	4	12.9%
	(*Teacher, Dick, Behind, That's Carry On*)		
	November	4	12.9%
	(*Camping, Up The Jungle, Henry, Matron*)		
3.	**October**	3	9.7%
	(*Jack, Don't Lose Your Head, Doctor*)		
4.	**February**	2	6.5%
	(*Cruising, Screaming*)		
	June	2	6.5%
	(*Follow That Camel, England*)		
	December	2	6.5%
	(*Nurse, Constable*)		
5.	**January**	1	3.2%
	(*Regardless*)		
	March	1	3.2%
	(*Spying*)		
	August	1	3.2%
	(*Cleo*)		
	September	1	3.2%
	(*Cowboy*)		
6.	**July**	0	0%

Spring	5	48.4%
Summer	3	9.7%
Autumn	8	25.8%
Winter	5	16.1%

Carry On Films
Month Film Released

1.	**November** (*Jack, Cleo, Cowboy, Girls, Emmannuelle*)	5	16.1%
	December (*Don't Lose Your Head, Doctor, At Your Convenience, Abroad, Behind*)	5	16.1%
2.	**February** (*Constable, Camping, Henry, That's Carry On*)	4	12.9%
	August (*Sergeant, Teacher, Screaming, Again Doctor*)	4	12.9%
3.	**March** (*Nurse, Regardless, Up The Jungle*)	3	9.7%
	September (*Follow That Camel, Up The Khyber, Loving*)	3	9.7%
4.	**June** (*Cabby, Spying*)	2	6.5%
	October (*England, Columbus*)	2	6.5%
5.	**April** (*Cruising*)	1	3.2%
	May (*Matron*)	1	3.2%
	July (*Dick*)	1	3.2%
6.	**January**	0	0%

Spring	5	16.1%
Summer	7	22.6%
Autumn	10	32.3%
Winter	9	29.0%

Carry On Films
Longest Film to be Released

Name of film	Finished Filming	Film Released	Months Taken
That's Carry On	April 1977	February 1978	10
Behind	April 1975	December 1975	8
At Your Convenience	May 1971	December 1971	7
Abroad	May 1972	December 1972	7
Screaming	February 1966	August 1966	6
Matron	November 1971	May 1972	6
Girls	May 1973	November 1973	6
Emmannuelle	May 1978	November 1978	6
Columbus	May 1992	October 1992	5
Teacher	April 1959	August 1959	4
Up The Khyber	May 1968	September 1968	4
Up The Jungle	November 1969	March 1970	4
Loving	May 1970	September 1970	4
England	June 1976	October 1976	4
Sergeant	May 1958	August 1958	3
Nurse	December 1958	March 1959	3
Spying	March 1964	June 1964	3
Cleo	August 1964	November 1964	3
Follow That Camel	June 1967	September 1967	3
Camping	November 1968	February 1969	3
Again Doctor	May 1969	August 1969	3
Henry	November 1970	February 1971	3
Dick	April 1974	July 1974	3
Constable	December 1959	February 1960	2
Regardless	January 1961	March 1961	2
Cruising	February 1962	April 1962	2
Cowboy	September 1965	November 1965	2
Don't Lose Your Head	October 1966	December 1966	2
Doctor	October 1967	December 1967	2
Cabby	May 1963	June 1963	1
Jack	October 1963	November 1963	1

Carry On Photography

	Film	Start Date	Finish Date	Days
1.	Jack	2.9.63	26.10.63	54
	Cowboy	12.7.65	3.9.65	54
	Follow That Camel	1.5.67	23.6.67	54
	Up The Khyber	8.4.68	31.5.68	54
2.	Regardless	28.11.60	17.1.61	51
3.	Matron	11.10.71	26.11.71	48
4.	Cleo	13.7.64	28.8.64	47
	Screaming	10.1.66	25.2.66	47
	Camping	7.10.68	22.11.68	47
	Henry	12.10.70	27.11.70	47
5.	Don't Lose Your Head	12.9.66	28.10.66	46
	Again Doctor	17.3.69	2.5.69	46
6.	At Your Convenience	22.3.71	7.5.71	45
7.	Cabby	25.3.63	7.5.63	43
8.	Doctor	11.9.67	20.10.67	41
9.	Sergeant	24.3.58	2.5.58	40
	Nurse	3.11.58	12.12.58	40
	Teacher	15.3.59	24.4.59	40
	Constable	9.11.59	18.12.59	40
	Cruising	8.1.62	16.2.62	40
	Up The Jungle	13.10.69	21.11.69	40
	Loving	6.4.70	15.5.70	40
	Abroad	17.4.72	26.5.72	40
	Girls	16.4.73	25.5.73	40
	Behind	10.3.75	18.4.75	40
10.	Dick	4.3.74	11.4.74	39
11.	Columbus	21.4.92	27.5.92	37
12.	Emmannuelle	10.4.78	15.5.78	36
13.	Spying	8.2.64	13.3.64	34
14.	England	3.5.76	4.6.76	33
15.	That's Carry On	?.4.77	?.4.77	None

Longest Carry On Film to Make

How long did it take to film a Carry On?

		Weeks	Days
1.	*Jack* (1963)	8	2
2.	*Follow That Camel* (1967)	7	4
	Up The Khyber (1968)	7	4
3.	*Cowboy* (1965)	7	3
4.	*Regardless* (1960)	6	6
5.	*Cleo* (1964)	6	4
	Screaming (1966)	6	4
	Don't Lose Your Head (1966)	6	4
	Camping (1968)	6	4
	Again Doctor (1967)	6	4
	Henry (1970)	6	4
	Matron (1971)	6	4
6.	*That's Carry On* (1977)	6	2
7.	*Cabby* (1963)	6	1
8.	*Constable* (1959)	5	6
	At Your Convenience (1971)	5	6
9.	*Doctor* (1967)	5	5
10.	*Sergeant* (1958)	5	4
	Nurse (1958)	5	4
	Teacher (1959)	5	4
	Cruising (1962)	5	4
	Loving (1970)	5	4
	Abroad (19720	5	4
	Girls (1973)	5	4
	Behind (1975)	5	4
11.	*Up The Jungle* (1969)	5	3
	Dick (1974)	5	3
12.	*Columbus* (1992)	5	1
13.	*Emmannuelle* (1978)	5	0
14.	*Spying* (1964)	4	5
15.	*England* (1976)	4	4

Longest Running Carry On Film

Listed below are the running times of the Carry On films and the length of the film used after they were edited. Each film reel contained 1,000 feet of film

		Running Time	*Length in Feet*
1.	*Screaming* (1966)	97	8,658
2.	*Follow That Camel* (1967)	95	8,550
	That's Carry On (1977)	95	8,524
	Cowboy (1965)	95	8,499
3.	*Doctor* (1967)	94	8,432
4.	*Cleo* (1964)	92	8,247
5.	*Cabby* (1963)	91	8,230
	Dick (1974)	91	8,201
	Columbus (1992)	91	8,176
	Jack (1963)	91	8,174
6.	*Don't Lose Your Head* (1966)	90	8,150
	Behind (1975)	90	8,139
	Regardless (1960)	90	8,124
	At Your Convenience (1971)	90	8,100
7.	*Henry* (1970)	89	8,046
	Again Doctor (1969)	89	8,010
	Up The Jungle (1969)	89	8,010
	Cruising (1962)	89	8,009
	England (1976)	89	8,000
8.	*Loving* (1970)	88	7,930
	Abroad (1972)	88	7,928
	Girls (1973)	88	7,921
	Camping (1968)	88	7,920
	Emmannuelle (1978)	88	7,916
	Up The Khyber (1968)	88	7,903
9.	*Matron* (1971)	87	7,871
	Spying (1964)	87	7,840
10.	*Constable* (1959)	86	7,781
	Nurse (1958)	86	7,771
	Teacher (1959)	86	7,771
11.	*Sergeant* (1958)	83	7,505

Longest Distance Travelled to Make a Carry-On Film

Listed below is the order in which the Carry On team travelled on location. Mileage calculated approximately as the crow flies.

1.	*Up The Khyber*	Snowdonia, North Wales	166 miles
2.	*Follow That Camel*	Camber Sands, Rye, Sussex	70 miles
3.	*At Your Convenience*	Brighton, Sussex	60 miles
	Girls	Brighton, Sussex	60 miles
4.	*Don't Lose Your Head*	Waddesdon Manor, Bucks	28 miles
5.	*Jack*	Frensham Ponds, Surrey	27 miles
	Columbus	Frensham Ponds, Surrey	27 miles
6.	*Sergeant*	Stoughton Guildford, Surrey	19 miles
7.	*Emmannuelle*	Wembley, North London	12 miles
8.	*Matron*	Ascot, Berkshire	11 miles
9.	*Teacher*	Ealing, West London	9.5 miles
	Constable	Ealing, West London	9.5 miles
10.	*Doctor*	Maidenhead Town Hall, Berks	9 miles
	Again Doctor	Maidenhead Town Hall, Berks	9 miles
	Behind	Maidenhead Town Hall, Berks	9 miles
11.	*Camping*	Northolt, Middlesex	8 miles
12.	*Regardless*	Park Street, Windsor, Berks	7 miles
	Cabby	Arthur Road, Windsor, Berks	7 miles
	Screaming	Arthur Road, Windsor, Berks	7 miles
	Loving	Arthur Road, Windsor, Berks	7 miles
	Henry	Long Walk, Windsor Castle, Berks	7 mles
13.	*Abroad*	Slough High Street, Berks	3 miles
14.	*Cowboy*	Black Park Fulmer, Bucks	2.5 miles
15.	*Dick*	St Mary's Church, Taplow, Bucks	2 miles
16.	*Nurse*	Iver Heath, Bucks	1 mile
17.	*Cruising*	Pinewood Studios	In grounds
	Spying	Pinewood Studios	In grounds
	Cleo	Pinewood Studios	In grounds
	Up The Jungle	Pinewood Studios	In grounds
	England	Pinewood Studios	In grounds
	That's Carry On	Pinewood Studios	In grounds

Carry On Casting

Below is a list of the number of people that appeared in each Carry On film.

	Film	Male	Female	Total
1.	*That's Carry On* (1977)	46	28	74
2.	*Regardless* (1960)	40	17	57
3.	*Columbus* (1992)	43	8	51
4.	*Sergeant* (1958)	45	5	50
5.	*Cowboy* (1965)	27	21	48
6.	*Nurse* (1958)	25	20	45
	Loving (1970)	27	18	45
	Emmannuelle (1978)	33	12	45
7.	*Up The Khyber* (1968)	21	21	42
	Behind (1975)	21	21	42
8.	*Cleo* (1964)	22	18	40
	Again Doctor (1969)	18	22	40
9.	*Follow That Camel* (1967)	23	15	38
	Doctor (1967)	21	17	38
10.	*Girls* (1973)	16	21	37
11.	*Constable* (1959)	21	15	36
	Spying (1964)	19	17	36
12.	*Camping* (1968)	14	20	34
	Henry (1970)	25	9	34
13.	*Matron* (1971)	14	19	33
	England (1976)	21	12	33
14.	*Dick* (1974)	21	11	32
15.	*Cabby* (1963)	19	12	31
	Don't Lose Your Head (1966)	16	15	31
16.	*Jack* (1963)	19	10	29
17.	*At Your Convenience* (1971)	16	11	27
18.	*Abroad* (1972)	16	10	26
19.	*Up The Jungle* (1969)	14	9	23
20.	*Cruising* (1962)	17	5	22
21.	*Screaming* (1966)	15	5	20
22.	*Teacher* (1959)	12	6	18

On Location (films)

After the film script was submitted and read, the location reckie accompanied by the Production Manager and Cameraman would seek out possible locations to use in the Carry On films. Once found, a report would be filed to Peter Rogers, the producer, who would decide if they were suitable for filming the external scene.

Most of the external location filming took place within a 15-mile radius of Pinewood Studios. For instance Black Park in Fulmer, a stones throw from the studios, were used in five different films. Locations such as Windsor and Maidenhead were used in no less than 11 of the films – over a third of the series. The furthest traveled on location by the team was to Snowdonia in North Wales, approximately 166 miles as the crow flies from Pinewood. The longest time spent on any location was 21 days (three weeks), which was to Camber Sands, Rye Sussex. Both of these were in the years 1967/68. There were some 68 journeys to external locations throughout the 31 films produced.

Of course all of the internal shots for the films were produced on the Sound Stages and in the Back Lot at Pinewood Studios.

The following pages include a comprehensive guide to all of the locations used in the making of the Carry On films.

The Rhododendron Walk (facing south) – Pinewood Studio Gardens. The scene was used in Carry On Henry *(1970), released in 1971*

Park Street in Windsor, scene used in Carry On Regardless *(1960),* Again Doctor *(1969) and* Loving *(1970)*

Courts shop in Maidenhead, scene used in Carry On Camping *(1968) The store closed it's doors in 2000*

Maidenhead Town Hall, scene used in Carry On Doctor *(1967),* Again Doctor *(1969) and* Behind *(1975), the town hall has now closed down*

CARRY ON MEMORY

"The person I remember best from the Carry Ons is Bernard Bresslaw who made his name mostly playing dim characters. He was far removed from that in real life. He thought nothing of finishing *The Times* crossword – the big one – in less than an hour. A delightful fellow with a great sense of humour. His early death robbed the theatre of a considerable actor who, in later life would have had a splendid career in the classics. He could have played practically any Shakespearean clown. I would love to have seen his Leah."

Harry Towb

League of Locations used in the Films

	Film	Number of times	% of times used
1.	*Camping* (1968)	8	8.1%
2.	*Dick* (1974)	7	7.1%
3.	*Constable* (1959)	6	6.1%
	Loving (1970)	6	6.1%
	Girls (1973)	6	6.1%
	Behind (1975)	6	6.1%
4.	*Cabby* (1963)	5	5.1%
	At Your Convenience (1971)	5	5.1%
5.	*Regardless* (1960)	4	4.0%
	Again Doctor (1969)	4	4.0%
	Abroad (1972)	4	4.0%
	Emmannuelle (1978)	4	4.0%
6.	*Sergeant* (1958)	3	3.0%
	Screaming (1966)	3	3.0%
	Don't Lose Your Head (1966)	3	3.0%
	Henry (1970)	3	3.0%
	Matron (1971)	3	3.0%
7.	*Nurse* (1958)	2	2.0%
	Spying (1964)	2	2.0%
	Cowboy (1965)	2	2.0%
	Up The Jungle (1970)	2	2.0%
	England (1976)	2	2.0%
8.	*Teacher* (1959)	1	1.0%
	Cruising (1962)	1	1.0%
	Jack (1963)	1	1.0%
	Cleo (1964)	1	1.0%
	Follow That Camel (1967)	1	1.0%
	Doctor (1967)	1	1.0%
	Up The Khyber (1968)	1	1.0%
	That's Carry On (1977)	1	1.0%
	Columbus (1992)	1	1.0%

Location Guide

Sergeant (1958) Locations used = 3
Church in opening wedding scene — Harefield Middlesex
Heathercrest National Service Depot — Queens Barracks, Stoughton, Guildford, Surrey
Closing scene as lorry leaves depot — Rear entrance to Pinewood

Nurse (1958) Locations used = 2
Ambulance travelling in opening scene — Streets of Iver Heath, Bucks
Haven Hospital — Rear of Pinewood Mansion

Teacher (1959) Locations used = 1
Maudlin Street School — Drayton Secondary School, Ealing, West London

Constable 1959 Location used = 6
Opening shot of Police Station — Hanwell, West London
Street Shots & Town Centre — Ealing, West London
Police on the March — Pinewood Green Estate
Department Store — F H Rowse, Ealing, West London
Post Office with K Williams & V Maddern — Manor Rd, Ealing, West London
Church Scene — Hanwell, West London

Regardless (1960) Locations used = 4
Helping Hands agency — Park Street, Windsor, Berks
K Williams collecting Yoki — 11 Clarence Road, Windsor
K Williams walking away from taxi — Thames St into Windsor Park
Railway Station — Winsor & Eton Railway St

Cruising (1962) Locations used = 1
Opening shots of Cruise Liner — Southampton Dock, Hants

Cabby (1963) Locations used = 5
Opening scenes of Sid James driving — Sheet Street, Windsor, Berks
Cab driving scenes — Pinewood Green Estate
Sid James & Jim Dale scene — Black Park Rd, Fulmer, Bucks
Street shots — Windsor, Berks
End chase scenes — Arthur Rd, Windsor, Berks

Jack (1963) Locations used = 1
Spanish coastline   Frensham Ponds, Surrey

Spying (1964) Locations used = 2
Opening scene of milk float   Rear entrance to Pinewood
Victor Maddern walking to lab   Hall of Fame and into the archive
                                                   department, Pinewood

Cleo (1964) Locations used = 1
Countryside scenes   Iver Heath, Bucks

Cowboy (1965) Locations used = 2
Horse & coach and fighting scenes   Chobham Common, Surrey
   "   "   "   "   "   Black Park, Fulmer, Bucks

Screaming (1966) Locations used = 3
Dr Watts house   Fulmer Grange, Fulmer, Bucks
Dan Dan toilets   South gates, Pinewood
Police Station   Windsor, Berks

Don't Lose Your Head (1966) Locations used = 3
Countryside scenes   Black Park, Fulmer Bucks
French Chateau   Waddesdon Manor, Bucks
Duel scene   Gardens at Pinewood

Follow That Camel (1967) Locations used = 1
Fort scenes   Camber Sands, Rye, Sussex

Doctor (1967) Locations used = 1
Hospital   Maidenhead Town Hall, St Ives Rd,
                                                   Berks

Up The Khyber (1968) Locations used = 1
Khyber Pass   Beddgelert, Snowdonia, North Wales

Camping (1968) Locations used = 8
Opening cinema scene   Gerrards Cross, Bucks
Camping shop scene   Courts, St Ives High St, Maidenhead,
                                                   Berks
The Potters house   Pinewood Green Cul-de-sac
Joan Sims house   Pinewood Green Estate

Josh Fiddler's Camp Site	Orchard at Pinewood
Campsite entrance	Juniper Cottages, Burnham Beeches, Bucks
Farmhouse	Glebe Farm Northolt , Middlesex
Coach trip to hostel	A412 Iver Heath to Slough

Again Doctor (1969) Locations used = 4

Long Hampton Hospital	Maidenhead Town Hall, St Ives Rd, Berks
Nursing Home	Iver Heath, Bucks
Dr Nookie's consulting rooms	Park Street, Windsor, Berks
Moore/Nookie clinic	Rear of Pinewood Mansion

Up The Jungle (1969) Locations used = 2

| Prof Tinkle's talk scene | The Village Hall, Fulmer, Bucks |
| Victorian Street | Alma Road, Windsor, Berks |

Loving (1970) Locations used = 6

Opening bus scene	Co-op roundabout, Slough, Berks
Shop window scene	Thames St Windsor, Berks
Wedded Bliss agency	12 Park St Windsor, Berks
Mr Snooper's house	45 Gloucester Sq, Windsor
Sid Bliss hails a cab	Windsor & Eton Railway St
32 Rogerham Mansions	Windsor, Berks

Henry (1970) — Locations used = 3

Farm where Henry chases wench to	Datchet, Berks
Horse scene	Long Walk, Windsor Castle
Countryside scenes	Black Park, Fulmer, Bucks

At Your Convenience (1971) Locations used = 5

Sid & Joan's houses	Pinewood Green Estate
Vic Spanner loses his trousers	Odeon Cinema, Uxbridge
Coach trip to Brighton	A412 Iver Heath to Slough
Hotel shot	The Palace Hotel, Brighton
Pier scenes	Palace Pier, Brighton

Matron (1971) Locations used = 3

Finisham Maternity Hospital	Heatherwood Hospital, Ascot, Berks
Sid & Gang driving along	Ascot High Street, Berks
Closing church scene	Denham Village, Bucks

Abroad (1972) Locations used = 4
Wundatours shop — High St, Slough, Berks
Elsbels hotel — Car Park at Pinewood
Dirt Rd leading to Elsbels — Bagshot, Surrey
Coach trip to Elsbels — A412 Iver Heath to Slough

Girls (1973) Locations used = 6
Council Hall — Town Hall, Slough, Berks
Platform & Train departing station — Marleybone Railway Station, London
Sid & Joan's hotel — Palace Hotel, Brighton
Fire Station scene — Fire Station, Windsor, Berks
Go-Kart scene — Palace Pier, Brighton, Sussex
Sid & Babs on Moped — B410 Slough to Datchet Rd

Dick (1974) Locations used = 7
Countryside scenes — Black Park, Fulmer, Iver Heath, Bucks; Maidenhead, Thickett, Berks
Rev Flasher's Church — St Mary's Church Hitcham, Bucks
Rev Flasher's home — Stoke Manor, Stoke Poges, Bucks
Prison — Constables Houses, Stoke Poges, Bucks
Horse chasing scenes — Langley Park, Berks

Behind (1975) Locations used = 6
University — Maidenhead Town Hall, St Ives Rd, Berks
Butchers shop scene — Farnham Common, Bucks
Bernie & Patsy's house — Pinewood Green Cul-de-sac
Countryside scenes — Iver Heath, Bucks
Camp Site — Orchard at Pinewood
Ian & Adrienne's — Pinewood Green Estate

England (1976) Locations used = 2
Army HQ — Rear of Pinewood Mansion
Army Barracks — Orchard at Pinewood

Emmannuelle (1978) Locations used = 4
Beryl & Larry's house — Pinewood Green Cul-de-sac
Laundrette — Bourne End, Bucks
Airport — Heathrow Airport, London
Others various scenes — London

That's Carry On (1977) **Locations used = 1**
K Williams & B Windsor   Projection Room, 7 Pinewood Studios

Columbus (1992) **Locations used = 1**
Sea/Coastal shots   Frensham Ponds, Surrey

Pinewood Green Estate used in Constable *(1959),*
Cabby *(1963),* Camping *(1968) and* At Your Convenience *(1971)*

St Mary's Church in the parish of Hitcham Taplow. The scene was used in Carry On Dick *(1974).*

Kissing Scenes seen in the edited Carry On films

1. *Emmannelle* (1978)   19
2. *Loving* (1970)   16
3. *Don't Lose Your Head* (1966) 14
4. *Henry* (1970)   9
   Abroad (1972)   9
5. *Nurse* (1958)   8
   Cabby (1963)   8
6. *Cleo* (1964)   7
   Up The Khyber (1968)   7
   At Your Convenience (1971) 7
   Girls (1973)   7
7. *Teacher* (1959)   6
   Screaming (1966)   6
   Matron (1971)   6
   England (1976)   6
8. *Jack* (1963)   5
9. *Constable* (1959)   4
   Regardless (1960)   4
   Cowboy (1965)   4
   Follow That Camel (1967)   4
   Doctor (1967)   4
   Up The Jungle (1969)   4
   Dick (1974)   4
   Behind (1975)   4
   Colombus (1992)   4
10. *Sergeant* (1958)   3
    Cruising (1962)   3
    Camping (1968)   3
11. *Again Doctor* (1969)   2
12. *Spying* (1964)   1

Scene used for the factory in Carry On At Your Convenience *(1971). It is situated behind the carpenter's workshops at Pinewood Studios*

Black Park Country Park, Fulmer, Bucks – scene used in Carry On Cowboy *(1965),* Don't Lose Your Head *(1966) and* Dick *(1974)*

Number 12 Park Street, Windsor, the house used for the Wedded Bliss agency in Loving *(1970). Below the railings is the stairway used in* Regardless *ten years earlier in 1960. Just think, the great Sid James once walked through this door!*

All Dressed up with Somewhere to go!

Over a span of thirty-four years the Carry On team dressed in costumes on nineteen occasions. Their very first outing in *Carry On Sergeant* (1958) saw them in army uniform (stand by your beds). Some eighteen years and twenty-seven films later they had come full circle and used the military uniform of the army again in *Carry On England* (1976).

One of the most popular costumes used was the nurse's uniform (*Cor!*). This was first seen in *Carry On Nurse* (1959) and went on to be used in three more of the series, *Carry On Doctor* (1967), *Carry On Again Doctor* (1969) and finally *Carry On Matron* (1971). There was to be another film – *Carry On Again Nurse* which was written by Norman Hudis and would have been the 30th anniversary film. It was due to be released in 1988, but never got to the production stage. This would have certainly capped an already brilliant medical era of the Carry On's.

In 1964 it was reportedly said that some of the set seen in the film *Cleopatra* was sold for a total of one hundred and fifty five pounds to the co-star of five Carry On films, Victor Maddern. He later loaned the very same set to another Pinewood Roman production for the sum of eight hundred pounds making a profit of six hundred and forty five pounds in the process!

"What a Carry On!"

CARRY ON MEMORY

"Working on *Carry On Nurse* was an absolute joy, very harmonious, a merry happy band of actors. The next *Carry On Teacher* was more problematic, not only was the work ludicrously rushed – but all the male leads were comedians or comics, and they were unable to communicate at all except by getting one up on each other by successive joke telling, maddening. Joan Sims once threatened to throw her lunch plate across the studio restaurant if another joke was told. No one took any notice – except me."

Rosalind Knight

Themes used in the films

Army (*Sergeant, Cleo, Up The Khyber, England*)	4	13.3%
Medical (*Nurse, Doctor, Again Doctor, Matron*)	4	13.3%
Holiday (*Cruising, Camping, Abroad*)	3	10.0%
Agency (*Regardless, Loving*)	2	6.7%
Teaching (*Teacher*)	1	3.3%
Police Force (*Constable*)	1	3.3%
Navy (*Jack*)	1	3.3%
Taxi Driver (*Cabby*)	1	3.3%
Espionage (*Spying*)	1	3.3%
Wild West (*Cowboy*)	1	3.3%
Horror (*Screaming*)	1	3.3%
French Revolution (*Don't Lose Your Head*)	1	3.3%
Foreign Legion (*Follow That Camel*)	1	3.3%
Big Game Hunters (*Up The Jungle*)	1	3.3%
Monarchy (*Henry*)	1	3.3%
Factory (*At Your Convenience*)	1	3.3%
Beauty Contest (*Girls*)	1	3.3%
Highwaymen (*Dick*)	1	3.3%
Archaeologists (*Behind*)	1	3.3%
Diplomats (*Emmannuelle*)	1	3.3%
Discovery (*Columbus*)	1	3.3%
Other	14	46.7%
Historical	9	30.0%
Medical	4	13.3%
Holiday	3	10.0%

Carry On Costumes

	Title		
1.	*Sergeant* (1958)	costume	modern
2.	*Nurse* (1958)	costume	modern
3.	*Teacher* (1959)		modern
4.	*Constable* (1959)	costume	modern
5.	*Regardless* (1960)		modern
6.	*Cruising* (1962)	costume	modern
7.	*Cabby* (1963)		modern
8.	*Jack* (1963)	period	
9.	*Spying* (1964)		modern
10.	*Cleo* (1964)	period	
11.	*Cowboy* (1965)	period	
12.	*Screaming* (1966)	period	
13.	*Don't Lose Your Head* (1966)	period	
14.	*Follow That Camel* (1967)	period	
15.	*Doctor* (1967)	costume	modern
16.	*Up The Khyber* (1968)	period	
17.	*Camping* (1968)		modern
18.	*Again Doctor* (1969)	costume	modern
19.	*Up The Jungle* (1969)	costume	modern
20.	*Loving* (1970)		modern
21.	*Henry* (19700	period	
22.	*At Your Convenience* (1971)		modern
23.	*Matron* (1971)	costume	modern
24.	*Abroad* (1972)		modern
25.	*Girls* (1973)		modern
26.	*Dick* (1974)	period	
27.	*Behind* (1975)		modern
28.	*England* (1976)	costume	
29.	*That's Carry On* (1977)	mixture	
30.	*Emmannuelle* (1978)		modern
31.	*Columbus* (1992)	period	

Carry On Wardrobe

The wardrobe used in the Carry On films

Wardrobe	Number	Percentage
Modern	11	35.5%
Period Costume	10	32.3%
Costume/Modern	8	25.8%
Costume	1	3.2%
Mixture	1	3.2%
	31	100%

The pathway leading to the gardens at Pinewood where scenes from Don't Lose Your Head *(1966),* Follow That Camel *(1967),* Up The Khyber *(1968) and* Henry *(1970) were filmed*

CARRY ON MEMORY

"I only have happy memories of the Carry On films. The main team all seemed very comfortable together and were very friendly to us. I remember putting my foot down about wearing a see through costume on *Carry On Dick* and the four of us 'win the day'!"

Laraine Humphreys

Have you been Registered?

PEG 1 is probably the number plate which mostly springs to mind from any of the Carry On films. It was one of nineteen used in *Carry On Cabby* in 1963, and was the crowning glory of Charlie Hawkins' Speedee Cab Company.

Obviously *Cabby* saw over a quarter of the vehicles used in the films. Ten of the films never used any registered vehicles, these of course being the historical, and the films based in foreign places.

It makes you wonder if any of the vehicles seen in the films are still in use today or in someone's private collection somewhere. I expect that a registration collector somewhere holds a number plate used from one of the Carry On films.

Back in 1994 one of the original London taxis (VLX 242) made it to Pinewood Studios and was photographed there, and later popped up on the inside back cover sleeve for a Carry On book – so they *are* still out there somewhere!

Look at the listed guide to those vehicles used in the films, and see if you know of the whereabouts of any!

CARRY ON MEMORIES

"My first appearance in a Carry On film was as a cabby in *Carry On Cabby*. At the audition when I was asked if I could drive I said yes, although I'd never been behind the wheel of a car in my life! I got the part but only had a fortnight to learn to drive! Full of nerves on my first day's filming on the Pinewood 'Back Lot' I discovered I had to drive fast towards the camera only turning at the last minute. The look on the camera man's face as I barely missed hitting him is something I shall remember all my life!"

Valerie Van Ost

* * * * * * * * *

"It was such a long time ago – but I remember the fun we had working on *Carry On Cabby*. The whole team were all so kind to me, especially Sid James."

Milo O'Shea

Carry On Films
Vehicle registrations seen in the films

1.	*Cabby*	19	25.3%
2.	*Constable*	7	9.3%
3.	*Loving*	6	8.0%
4.	*Camping*	5	6.7%
	At Your Convenience	5	6.7%
	Matron	5	6.7%
5.	*Sergeant*	4	5.3%
	Behind	4	5.3%
6.	*Screaming*	3	4.0%
	Again Doctor	3	4.0%
	Girls	3	4.0%
7.	*Regardless*	2	2.7%
	England	2	2.7%
	Emmannuelle	2	2.7%
8.	*Nurse*	1	1.3%
	Teacher	1	1.3%
	Spying	1	1.3%
	Doctor	1	1.3%
	Abroad	1	1.3%

total of 75 vehicles seen in 19 films

An overall average of almost 4 vehicles per film.

Pinewood Road used in Carry On Nurse *where the ambulance 705 CPP was driven down in 1958*

Vehicle registration plates used in
The Carry On films

Sergeant (1958) = total of 4 seen in the film
R7234660	Army lorry
XMY 636	Old style sports car
81 BP 39	Army lorry
EMV 675	Laundry van

Nurse (1958) = total of 1 seen in the film
| 705 CPP | Ambulance |

Teacher (1959) = total of 1 seen in the film
| 373 THE | Car outside of the school |

Constable (1959) = total of 7 seen in film
YDU 212	Triumph sports car
892 FPC	Austin Cambridge Police car
UUV 133	Austin Cambridge Police car
WLU 545	Wages van
AGT 547	Robber's car
285 BH	Tow truck
JHU 319	Police van (black mariah)

Regardless (1960) = total of 2 seen in film
| 353 HPP | Rolls Royce (black) |
| TUW 793 | London taxi FX2 |

Cabby (1963) = total of 19 seen in film
VLA 161	London taxi FX2
UYR 137	London taxi FX2
806 MHU	Lambretta Scooter
MOW 872	London taxi FX2
MCJ 173	London taxi FX2
PEG 1	Old style London taxi
WYL 607	London taxi FX2
OWC 167	Ford Cortina Mk1
SGK 473	London taxi FX2
OWC 166	Ford Cortina Mk1
LXA 477	London taxi FX2
726 MRJ	London taxi FX2

OWC 170	Ford Cortina Mk1
OWC 172	Ford Cortina Mk1
OWC 165	Ford Cortina Mk1
OWC 154	Ford Cortina Mk1
CB 6	Jaguar
TLH 595	London taxi FX2
VLX 242	London taxi FX2

Spying (1964) = total of 1 seen in film
| 235 HLC | Milk float |

Screaming (1966) = total of 3 seen in film
HS 25	Police car
X 285	Dr Watts' car
MO 1480	Taxi

Doctor (1967) = total of 1 seen in film
| MBF 979 | Ambulance |

Camping (1968) = total of 5 seen in film
FYB 352D	Vauxhall Viva van
725 PHD	Ford Zephur Mk 1
JJM 737F	Coach
CLY 214E	Mini Moke
GWJ 575B	Taxi

Again Doctor (1969) = total of 3 seen in film
SLW 542	Rolls Royce (black)
VLP 687G	London taxi FX2
WMF 930G	Rolls Royce (white)

Loving (1970) = total of 6 seen in film
NNC 730H	Austin Mini
BGJ 141B	London taxi FX2
AGU 756G	London taxi FX2
YUC 306H	London taxi FX2
SLF 700F	London taxi FX2
NOY 650E	London taxi FX2

At Your Convenience (1971) = total of 5 seen in film
WXF 584	Sid's car
RON 759G	Ford Capri Mk 2
VOP 346J	Triumph sports car

VLK 889G	Ford escort van
ONM 871H	Coach

Matron (1971) = total of 5 seen in film

CBH 159B	Ford Zephur Mk 2
100 BYV	Rolls Royce (black)
983 ETT	London taxi FX2
BPP 425K	Ambulance
437 BXA	Ambulance

Abroad (1972) = total of 1 seen in film

M76242	Coach

Girls (1973) = total of 3 seen in film

FYC 530J	Van outside of the hotel
YSF 557L	Fire engine
RGX 44L	Moped

Behind (1975) = total of 4 seen in film

LMV 365K	Austin 1300
MMU 533G	Jaguar
VMY 488G	Archaeologist van
XPP 226J	Triumph sports car

England (1976) = total of 2 seen in film

M198274	Army truck
334 PML	Army car

Emmannuelle (1978) = total of 2 seen in film

OP 55R	Rolls Royce (black)
KLT 144P	Triumph TR6

The A412 Slough to Iver Heath road, where the coach scenes for Camping *(1968),* At Your Convenience *(1971) and* Abroad *(1972) were filmed*

Names used in the films

Over the thirty films produced, excluding the compilation film *That's Carry On* (1977), the name Potter was used five times in four films, making it the most common name used. The name Potter first appeared in *Constable* (1960) scripted for Leslie Phillips who played Tom Potter (there's nothing hotter) – really!

There then came a gap of six years before it cropped up again, this time as the Albert Potter played by the versatile actor Jim Dale in *Screaming* (1966), the boyfriend of that Mann Doris, played by Angela Douglas.

In October 1968 *Camping* saw its production on where Terry Scott and Betty Marsden played the campoholics Peter and Harriet Potter (on a bicycle made for two).

The final time the name was used was in *Girls* (1973), on where Peter Potter was scripted for the second time, now played by the gentle giant of the team Bernard Bresslaw, Sid's publicity agent.

Talking of the legend Sid James, he actually used his own Christian name six times, in six films, in six years, starting with *Up The Khyber* (1968) on where he played Sir Sidney Ruff-Diamond, through to Sidney Fiddler in *Girls* (1973). In between came Sid Boggle *Camping* (1968), Sidney Bliss *Loving* (1970), Sid Plummer *At Your Convenience* (1971) and Sid Carter in *Matron* (1971), where Hattie Jacques played her last role as matron.

Over a span of thirteen years, the larger than life Hattie played the matron on four occasions, obviously in the medical farces starting way back in 1958 with *Nurse*, again nine years later in *Doctor* (1967), through to *Again Doctor* (1969) and finally in *Matron* (1971).

In an interview at Pinewood Studios on 30th May 1999, Peter Rogers the producer of all the Carry Ons said that no stars name ever appeared above the title Carry On. The Carry On name was the star.

CARRY ON MEMORY

"I do remember how nervous I was my first day on a Carry On set, until the lovely Kenneth Williams, understanding how I was feeling, screamed from one end of the hospital ward 'Oh yes, you don't want to know me now, do you?' and greeted me like an old friend (which I wasn't). It broke the ice and I loved him for it."

Marianne Stone

What The Carry On films Cost To Make

1.	*Sergeant* (1958)	£74,000
2.	*Nurse* (1958)	£71,000
3.	*Teacher* (1959)	£78,000
4.	*Constable* (1959)	£82,500*
5.	*Regardless* (1960)	£100,000
6.	*Cruising* (1962)	£140,000
7.	*Cabby* (1963)	£149,986
8.	*Jack* (1963)	£152,000*
9.	*Spying* (1964)	£148,000*
10.	*Cleo* (1964)	£194,323
11.	*Cowboy* (1965)	£195,000*
12.	*Screaming* (1966)	£197,500*
13.	*Don't Lose Your Head* (1966)	£200,000
14.	*Follow That Camel* (1967)	£288,366
15.	*Doctor* (1967)	£214,000*
16.	*Up The Khyber* (1968)	£260,000*
17.	*Camping* (1968)	£208,354
18.	*Again Doctor* (1969)	£219,000*
19.	*Up The Jungle* (1969)	£210,000*
20.	*Loving* (1970)	£215,000*
21.	*Henry* (1970)	£223,000
22.	*At Your Convenience* (1971)	£220,000*
23.	*Matron* (1971)	£224,995
24.	*Abroad* (1972)	£225,000*
25.	*Girls* (1973)	£205,962
26.	*Dick* (1974)	£245,000*
27.	*Behind* (1975)	£217,000*
28.	*England* (1976)	£250,000
29.	*That's Carry On* (1977)	£30,000*
30.	*Emmannuelle* (1978)	£320,000
31.	*Columbus* (1992)	£2,500,000

* Denotes an estimated calculation

Joan 38 Sims

Kenneth 31 Connor

Peter 32 Butterworth

Sid 29 James

Jack 28 Douglas

Barbara 27 Windsor

Kenneth 27 Williams

Chapter 2
The Team

Charles 26 Hawtrey

Bernard 25 Bresslaw

Hattie 18 Jacques

Jim 1 Dale

Patsy 11 Rowlands

Terry 10 Scott

Who did it and when?

The mainstay Carry On team consisted of thirteen regulars. These included Kenneth Connor, Peter Butterworth, Bernard Bresslaw, Jim Dale, Jack Douglas, Terry Scott, Patsy Rowlands and the larger than life Hattie Jacques.

We the viewers saw Kenneth Williams star in twenty-six of the thirty-one films making him the team member with the most appearances. Charles Hawtrey appeared in the most-number films in the least number of years – in fact he was seen in twenty-three films in fifteen years and it was reported that he could have appeared in other Carry On films, but constant rivalry over top billing put paid to this. Of course Joan Sims was the lady we all loved after seeing her star in twenty-one consecutive out of the twenty-four she appeared in. This not only made Joan top female film performer but also gave her the rating of top overall appearances throughout the Carry On film, television and stage productions combined. This amounted to a massive thirty-eight in total.

When thinking of the Carry Ons Barbara Windsor (along with a few others) always comes to mind; her ten film performances must have been memorable as eleven other team members actually made more films.

The most famous name to grace the Carry Ons was the lovable Sid James who appeared in twenty of the films. His rugged exterior was instantly recognizable to the fans and his name is still well-known today, many years after his untimely death.

"Stop Messin' About!"

Keep the Carry On flag flying! Authors and Broadcasters Morris Bright and Robert Ross after another successful event at Pinewood Studios taken on 29th April 2001

The Carry On Team – What were they in?

Bernard Bresslaw
And in my Lady's Chamber, Abroad, Again Christmas, At Your Convenience, Behind, Camping, Christmas 1969, 1973, Cowboy, Dick, Doctor, Follow That Camel, Girls, London, Loving, Matron, Screaming, Up The Jungle, Up The Khyber, Lamp Posts of the Empire, Short Knight, Long Daze, Under the Round Table, What a Carry On, Who Needs Kitchener, Wot a Carry On in Blackpool.

Peter Butterworth
And in my Lady's Chamber, Abroad, Again Doctor, The Baron Outlook, Behind, Camping, Christmas 1969, 1972, 1973, Cowboy, Dick, Doctor, Don't Lose Your Head, Emmannuelle, England, Follow That Camel, Girls, Henry, Laughing, London, Loving, Screaming, Up The Khyber, The Case of the Coughing Parrot, The Case of the Screaming Winkles, Lamp Posts of the Empire, The Prisoner of Spenda, Short Knight, Long Daze, The Sobbing Cavalier, Under the Round Table, What a Carry On!

Kenneth Connor
And in my Lady's Chamber, Abroad, Again Christmas, The Baron Outlook, Behind, Cabby, Christmas 1972, 1973, Cleo, Constable, Cruising, Dick, Emmannuelle, England, Girls, Henry, Laughing, London, Matron, Nurse, Regardless, Sergeant, Teacher, Up The Jungle, The Case of the Coughing Parrot, The Case of the Screaming Winkles, Lamp Posts of the Empire, The Nine Old Cobblers, Norbet Smith – A Life, One in the Eye for Harold, Orgy and Bess, The Prisoner of Spenda, Short Knight, Long Daze, Under the Round Table, What a Carry On!, Who Needs Kitchener.

Jim Dale
Again Doctor, Cabby, Cleo, Colombus, Cowboy, Doctor, Don't Lose Your Head, Follow That Camel, Jack, Screaming, Spying.

Jack Douglas
And in my Lady's Chamber, Abroad, Behind, Christmas 1972, 1973, Colombus, Dick, Emmannuelle, England, Girls, Laughing, London, Matron, The Case of the Coughing Parrot, The Case of the Screaming Winkles, Lamp Posts of the Empire, The Nine Old Cobblers, Norbet Smith – A Life, One in the Eye for Harold, Orgy and Bess, The Prisoner of Spenda, Short Knight, Long Daze, The Sobbing Cavalier, Under the Round Table, What a Carry On!, Who Needs Kitchener.

Charles Hawtrey
Abroad, Again Christmas, Again Doctor, At Your Convenience, Cabby, Camping, Christmas 1969, Cleo, Constable, Cowboy, Doctor, Don't Lose Your Head, Follow That Camel, Henry, Jack, Loving,

	Matron, Nurse, Regardless, Screaming, Sergeant, Spying, Teacher, Up The Jungle, Up The Khyber.
Hattie Jacques	*Abroad, Again Doctor, At Your Convenience, Cabby, Camping, Christmas 1969, 1972, Constable, Dick, Doctor, Loving, Matron, Nurse, Regardless, Sergeant, Teacher, Orgy and Bess.*
Sid James	*Abroad, Again Christmas, Again Doctor, At Your Convenience, The Baron Outlook, Cabby, Camping, Christmas 1969, 1973, Cleo, Constable, Cowboy, Cruising, Dick, Doctor, Don't Lose Your Head, Girls, Henry, London, Loving, Matron, Regardless, Sid, Up The Jungle, Up The Khyber, Orgy and Bess, The Prisoner of Spenda, The Sobbing Cavalier, What a Carry On!*
Patsy Rowlands	*Abroad, Again Doctor, At Your Convenience, Behind, Dick, Girls, Henry, Loving, Matron, The Nine Old Cobblers.*
Terry Scott	*Again Christmas, Camping, Christmas 1969, Henry, Loving, Matron, Sergeant, Up The Jungle, Up The Khyber.*
Joan Sims	*And in my Lady's Chamber, Abroad, Again Doctor, At Your Convenience, The Baron Outlook, Behind, Camping, Christmas 1972, 1973, Cleo, Constable, Cowboy, Dick, Doctor, Don't Lose Your Head, Emmannelle, England, Follow That Camel, Girls, Henry, Loving, Matron, Nurse, Regardless, Screaming, Teacher, Up The Jungle, Up The Khyber, The Case of the Coughing Parrot, The Case of the Screaming Winkles, The Nine Old Cobblers, One in the Eye for Harold, The Prisoner of Spenda, Short Knight, Long Daze, The Sobbing Cavalier, Under the Round Table, Who Needs Kitchener.*
Kenneth Williams	*Abroad, Again Doctor, At Your Convenience, Behind, Camping, Cleo, Constable, Cowboy, Cruising, Dick, Doctor, Don't Lose Your Head, Emmannuelle, Follow That Camel, Henry, Jack, Laughing's Christmas Classics, Loving, Matron, Nurse, Regardless, Screaming, Sergeant, Spying, Teacher, Up The Khyber, Thats Carry On.*
Barbara Windsor	*And in my Lady's Chamber, Abroad, Again Christmas, Again Doctor, Barbara, The Baron Outlook, Camping, Christmas 1969, 1972, 1973, Dick, Doctor, Girls, Henry, Laughing, Christmas Classics, London, Matron, Spying, Up Yer Cinders, Lamp Posts of the Empire, The Nine Old Cobblers, Norbet Smith – A Life, Orgy and Bess, The Prisoner of Spenda, The Sobbing Cavalier, Thats Carry On, What a Carry On!, Who Needs Kitchener, Wot a Carry On in Blackpool.*

The Stars and Co-stars' First & Last Films

Over a period of thirty-four years and thirty-one films, have you ever wondered what the members of this famous teams' first and last films were? Now you know…

Team Member	First film	Last film
Charles Hawtrey	*Sergeant* (1958)	*Abroad* (1972)
Kenneth Williams	*Sergeant* (1958)	*Emmannuelle* (1978)
Hattie Jacques	*Sergeant* (1958)	*Dick* (1974)
Kenneth Connor	*Sergeant* (1958)	*Emmannuelle* (1978)
Terry Scott	*Sergeant* (1958)	*Matron* (1971)
Shirley Eaton	*Sergeant* (1958)	*Constable* (1959)
Joan Sims	*Nurse* (1958)	*Emmannuelle* (1978)
Leslie Phillips	*Nurse* (1958)	*Columbus* (1992)
Sid James	*Constable* (1959)	*Dick* (1974)
Joan Hickson	*Constable* (1959)	*Girls* (1973)
Liz Fraser	*Regardless* (1960)	*Behind* (1975)
David Lodge	*Regardless* (1960)	*England* (1976)
Dilys Laye	*Cruising* (1962)	*Camping* (1968)
Jim Dale	*Cabby* (1963)	*Columbus* (1992)
Peter Gilmore	*Cabby* (1963)	*Columbus* (1992)
Bernard Cribbins	*Jack* (1963)	*Columbus* (1992)
Barbara Windsor	*Spying* (1964)	*Dick* (1974)
Hugh Futcher	*Spying* (1964)	*Behind* (1975)
Jon Pertwee	*Cleo* (1964)	*Columbus* (1992)
Bernard Bresslaw	*Cowboy* (1965)	*Behind* (1975)
Peter Butterworth	*Cowboy* (1965)	*Emmannuelle* (1978)
Angela Douglas	*Cowboy* (1965)	*Up The Khyber* (1968)
Julian Holloway	*Follow That Camel* (1967)	*England* (1976)
Valerie Leon	*Up The Khyber* (1968)	*Girls* (1973)
Patsy Rowlands	*Again Doctor* (1969)	*Behind* (1975)
Jacki Piper	*Up The Jungle* (1969)	*Matron* (1971)
Richard O'Callaghan	*Loving* (1970)	*At Your Convenience* (1971)
Jack Douglas	*Matron* (1971)	*Columbus* (1992)

CARRY ON MEMORIES

"My biggest memory is of *Carry On Camping* when I was so cold that they had to spray the ground with green paint to look like grass and fix leaves to the trees. Also this was the film that Barbara Windsor and I became friends, which led on to me doing *Wild Wild Women* for BBC TV and ultimately to me getting *On The Buses* – we have remained good friends ever since."

Anna Karen

****

"I appeared in two Carry On films *Again Doctor* and *Up The Jungle*. I was only a small cog in a much bigger wheel, however the cast of the two films I worked on were lovely people who showed much kindness to a novice, especially Sid James."

Heather Emmanuel

****

"My memory of working on the Carry On films – one only – *Carry On England* was one of disappointment. I was disappointed that I had not appeared in them earlier! There was a great atmosphere on the set – both with the crew and artistes. It wasn't like work. It was fun, fun, fun – all the way. To top it all, I was working with my very own Sergeant Major – Windsor Davies."

Melvyn Hayes

The gardens of fragrance where Kenneth Williams and Sid James fought their duel in Carry On Don't Lose Your Head *(1966)*

Carry-on League of Stars & Co-Stars starring in the Films

		No. Films	% of Films
1.	Kenneth Williams	26	83.9%
2.	Joan Sims	24	77.4%
3.	Charles Hawtrey	23	74.2%
4.	Sid James	19	61.3%
5.	Kenneth Connor	17	54.8%
6.	Peter Butterworth	16	51.6%
7.	Hattie Jacques	14	45.2%
	Bernard Bresslaw	14	45.2%
8.	Michael Nightingale	12	38.7%
9.	Jim Dale	10	32.3%
	Peter Gilmore	10	32.3%
	Barbara Windsor	10	32.3%
10.	Patsy Rowlands	9	29.0%
	Marianne Stone	9	29.0%
11.	Jack Douglas	8	25.8%
	Julian Holoway	8	25.8%
12.	Terry Scott	7	22.6%
	Cyril Chamberlain	7	22.6%
	Gertan Klaber	7	22.6%
	Frank Forsyth	7	22.6%
	Hugh Futcher	7	22.6%
	Billy Cornelius	7	22.6%
	Lucy Griffiths	7	22.6%
13.	Tom Clegg	6	19.4%
	Sally Douglas	6	19.4%
	Valerie Leon	6	19.4%
	Margeret Nolan	6	19.4%
	Brian Osborne	6	19.4%
	Derek Francis	6	19.4%
	Simon Cain	6	19.4%
14.	Victor Maddern	5	16.1%
	Bill Maynard	5	16.1%
	Alexandra Dane	5	16.1%

Peter Gilmore
Peter, of the Onedian Line *fame in the '70s, crops up in a third of all the Carry On films made. He fitted in well with the team and his versatility is shown by his playing a number of different characters*

Hugh Futcher
Hugh first appeared in Carry On Spying *in 1964. He can be seen lying on his bed of nails in the Kasbah. Hugh went on to star in another six films, his last being a painter in* Carry On Behind *(1975). Once seen, his face was never forgotten – especially by Carry On fans*

	Joan Hickson	5	16.1%
	David Lodge	5	16.1%
	Norman Mitchell	5	16.1%
	Valerie Shute	5	16.1%
	Michael Ward	5	16.1%
	Anthony Sagar	5	16.1%
	Amelia Bayntun	5	16.1%
15.	Esma Cannon	4	12.9%
	Julian Orchard	4	12.9%
	Leslie Philips	4	12.9%
	Terence Longdon	4	12.9%
	Jacki Piper	4	12.9%
	Eric Barker	4	12.9%
	Larry Dann	4	12.9%
	Angela Douglas	4	12.9%
	Liz Fraser	4	12.9%
	Dilys Laye	4	12.9%
	Bill Owen	4	12.9%
	Brian Oulton	4	12.9%
	Jon Pertwee	4	
	June Whitfield	4	
	Ian Wilson	4	
	Jeremy Connor	4	
	Valerie Van Ost	4	
16.	Bernard Cribbins	3	
	Shirley Eaton	3	
	Judith Furse	3	
	Angela Grant	3	
	Linda Hooks	3	
	Rennee Houston	3	
	Harry Locke	3	9.7%
	Brian Rowlinson	3	9.7%
	Norman Rossington	3	9.7%
	Jimmy Thomson	3	9.7%
	Johnny Briggs	3	9.7%
	Ed Devereaux	3	9.7%
	Leon Greene	3	9.7%
	Dominique Don	3	9.7%
	Vicki Smith	3	9.7%
17.	Frankie Howerd	2	6.5%
	Amanda Barrie	2	6.5%
	Norman Chappel	2	6.5%
	Kenneth Cope	2	6.5%

Liz Fraser
Liz starred in four Carry On films. The first was Regardless *(1960) and* Cruising, Cabby *and* Behind *followed over the next 15 years. Her last Carry On appearance was in the stage show* Carry On Laughing *with the Slimming Factory, which ran on the 1975 Scarborough summer season. Jack Douglas, Kenneth Connor and Peter Butterworth also appeared. Liz is an excellent actress who has appeared in many other films and TV roles*

Richard O'Callaghan
Richard was a new face brought into the team for Carry In Loving *(1970). He starred in two films, working closely with Jacki Piper on both occasions*

Shirley Eaton
Shirley starred in three of the early Carry Ons adding a touch of glamour to the team. She actually ranks at number two behind Charles Hawtrey in the overall ratios, as she made three Carry Ons in two years

Alan Curtis	2	6.5%
Windsor Davis	2	6.5%
Fennella Fielding	2	6.5%
Carol Hawkins	2	6.5%
Rosalind Knight	2	6.5%
Jimmy Logan	2	6.5%
Wendy Richard	2	6.5%
Elspeth March	2	6.5%
Betty Marsden	2	6.5%
Freddie Mills	2	6.5%
Bill Pertwee	2	6.5%
Eric Pohlmann	2	6.5%
Anton Rodgers	2	6.5%
John Carlin	2	6.5%
Peter Boita	2	6.5%
Vincent Ball	2	6.5%
Patrick Cargill	2	6.5%
Pat Coombs	2	6.5%
Sally Geeson	2	6.5%
Irene Handl	2	6.5%
Anita Harris	2	6.5%
Richard O'Callaghan	2	6.5%
Percy Herbert	2	6.5%
Peter Jones	2	6.5%
Noel Dyson	2	6.5%
Ambrosine Phillpotts	2	6.5%
June Jago	2	6.5%
Gilly Grant	2	6.5%
Anna Karen	2	6.5%
Alan Curtis	2	6.5%
John Clive	2	6.5%
Ian Whittaker	2	6.5%
Hilda Fenemore	2	6.5%
David Williams	2	6.5%
Leigh Madison	2	6.5%
Laraine Humphreys	2	6.5%
Philip Stone	2	6.5%
John Antrobus	2	6.5%
18. Roy Castle	1	3.2%
Harry H Corbett	1	3.2%
Suzanne Danielle	1	3.2%
William Hartnell	1	3.2%
Imogen Hassel	1	3.2%
Sherrie Hewson	1	3.2%

Alexandra Dane
Alexandra was first seen as an instructor in Carry on Doctor *(1967), putting Charles Hawtrey through his maternity exercises. She starred in three more films and finally, in 1975, was seen in a low-cut dress in Carry on Behind. Cor!*

Valerie Leon
Tall, beautiful and glamorous. These three words describe this star of six Carry On films. Valerie owned an Austin GT with the number plate VL1 in the early '70s. She is still as beautiful now as when the fans saw her in the films

Fenella Fielding
Fenella starred in two films, Regardless *(1960) and* Screaming *in 1966, which was undoubtedly one of the finest performances in the entire series. She is an approachable lady and always has time for her fans*

Wilfred Hyde-White	1	3.2%
Diane Langton	1	3.2%
Warren Mitchell	1	3.2%
Bob Monkhouse	1	3.2%
Lance Percival	1	3.2%
Ted Ray	1	3.2%
Dany Robin	1	3.2%
Phil Silvers	1	3.2%
Elke Sommer	1	3.2%
Penelope Keith	1	3.2%
Ian Lavender	1	3.2%
George Layton	1	3.2%
Kenny Lynch	1	
Michael Medwin	1	
Juliet Mills	1	
Patrick Mower	1	
Dandy Nicholls	1	
Milo O'Shea	1	
Richard O'Sullivan	1	
Cecil Parker	1	
Nicolas Parsons	1	
Beryl Reid	1	
Arnold Ridley	1	
Cardew Robinson	1	
Frank Thornton	1	
Dora Bryan	1	3.2%
Terence Alexander	1	3.2%
Robin Askwith	1	3.2%
Wilfred Brambell	1	3.2%
Ray Brooks	1	3.2%
Marc Sinden	1	3.2%
Jeremy Desmonde	1	3.2%
Judy Geeson	1	3.2%
Deryck Guyler	1	3.2%
Sheila Hancock	1	3.2%
Melvyn Hayes	1	3.2%
Patricia Hayes	1	3.2%
Donald Hewlett	1	3.2%
Donald Houston	1	3.2%
Geoffrey Hughes	1	3.2%
Jill Ireland	1	3.2%
Christine Ozane	1	3.2%
Michael Balfour	1	3.2%
Susan Shaw	1	3.2%

Frank Thornton
Frank only appeared in one Carry On – Screaming *in 1966. He played Mr Jones, manager of the shop the dummy was stolen from. He went on to Captain Peacock fame in* Are You Being Served *and can be seen today in* Last of the Summer Wine

Marc Sinden
Marc is the son of Sir Donald. He co-starred in the final film of the series, Carry On Columbus *(1992) as Captain Perez. Marc once said "he was honoured to have appeared in a Carry On film". He now runs his own production company.*

Christine Ozanne
Christine's only Carry On role was in Nurse, *made in 1958 and released in 1959. She can be seen cleaning the hospital in the background on a couple of occasions. She now runs her own Shakespeare touring company.*

Gerald Campion	1	3.2%
Ronnie Stevens	1	3.2%
Richard O'Brien	1	3.2%
Bob Todd	1	3.2%
Bill Kenwright	1	3.2%
Mike Grady	1	3.2%
Olga Lowe	1	3.2%
Elizabeth Knight	1	3.2%
David Kernan	1	3.2%

CARRY ON MEMORIES

"Camping as everyone knows was made in November – in a field – at Pinewood. Wearing very little, Joan Sims and I were freezing and constantly damp – however it is one of my happiest memories working with Joan, Sid and Bernie, we laughed a lot and played a lot of poker in between showers! There was also of course the constant spraying of the leaves 'green' and the midges rose at 5 pm to bite us on the legs – but we loved it!"

Dilys Laye

* * * * * * * * * *

"In *Carry On Loving* full-size real cream cakes were thrown smack into my face. After each take my blouse had to be washed then dried with a hairdryer, my make-up reapplied, and the gunge combed out of my rather expensive hairpiece ready for the next cake to be thrown by Gerald Thomas. My skin was tingling by the end of the day and I haven't been able to look a cream cake in the face since."

Valerie Shute

* * * * * * * * * *

"*Carry On England* was one of my first film jobs as a new actress. I remember clearly how helpful Kenneth Connor was to me. He gave his valuable professional time to help me learn how to be funny on camera. I was lucky enough to work with him again, when he joined the cast in *Hi De Hi*. I think he was generous with his talent and cared about people and team work."

Linda Regan

Sustained Appearances in Carry-On Films

These are the top ten sustained appearances in the Carry On film series by the stars with out missing one. (All statistics compiled from 1958 to 1992.)

1.	Joan Sims from *Cleo* (1964) to *Emmannuelle* (1978)	21	67.7%
2.	Charles Hawtrey from *Cabby* (1963) to *Matron* (1971)	18	58.0%
3.	Sid James *Doctor* (1967) to *Dick* (1974)	12	38.7%
4.	Kenneth Williams from *Jack* (1963) to *Camping* (1968)	11	35.5%
5.	Jack Douglas from *Abroad* (1972) to *Columbus* (1992)	9	29.0%
	Jim Dale from *Cabby* (1963) to *Doctor* (1967)	9	29.0%
6.	Kenneth Connor from *Abroad* (1972) to *Emmannuelle* (1978)	8	25.8%
	Patsy Rowlands from *Loving* (1970) to *Behind* (1975)	8	25.8%
	Peter Butterworth from *Cowboy* (1965) to *Camping* (1968)	8	25.8%
7.	Bernard Bresslaw from *At Your Convenience* (1971) to *Behind* (1975)	6	19.4%
8.	Hattie Jacques from *Sergeant* (1958) to *Regardless* (1960)	5	16.1%
9.	Terry Scott from *Camping* (1968) to *Henry* (1970)	4	12.9%
	Barbara Windsor from *Abroad* (1972) to *Dick* (1974)	4	12.9%
	Esma Cannon from *Constable* (1959) to *Cabby* (1963)	4	12.9%
10.	Leslie Phillips from *Nurse* (1958) to *Constable* (1959)	3	9.7%
	Liz Fraser from *Regardless* (1960) to *Cabby* (1963)	3	9.7%

Carry-On Ratio's

This list below shows the stars and how many Carry On films they appeared in over a number of years. Figures do not include the *That's Carry On* (1977) compilation and *Columbus* (1992).

1.	Charles Hawtrey	23 films in 15 years	65.2%
2.	Shirley Eaton	3 films in 2 years	66.6%
3.	Jim Dale	10 films in 7 years	70.0%
4.	Patsy Rowlands	9 films in 7 years	77.7%
5.	Bernard Bresslaw	14 films in 11 years	78.6%
6.	Joan Sims	24 films in 20 years	83.3%
7.	Kenneth Williams	25 films in 21 years	84.0%
8.	Sidney James	19 films in 16 years	84.2%
9.	Peter Butterworth	16 films in 14 years	87.5%
10.	Jack Douglas	7 films in 7 years	100.0%
	Valerie Leon	6 films in 6 years	100.0%
	Angela Douglas	4 films in 4 years	100.0%
	Jacki Piper	4 films in 4 years	100.0%
11.	Hattie Jacques	14 films in 16 years	114.2%
12.	Barbara Windsor	9 films in 11 years	122.2%
13.	Kenneth Connor	17 films in 21 years	123.5%
14.	Julian Holloway	8 films in 10 years	125.0%
15.	Hugh Futcher	7 films in 12 years	171.4%
16.	Dilys Laye	4 films in 7 years	175.0%
17.	Terry Scott	7 films in 15 years	214.2%
	29 films made in 21 years		72.4%

How many scenes the stars were seen in the edited version of the films

Sergeant (1958)

Kenneth Connor	38
Charles Hawtrey	24
Kenneth Williams	22
Hattie Jacques	9
Terry Scott	2

Nurse (1958)

Kenneth Connor	30
Kenneth Williams	30
Joan Sims	23
Hattie Jacques	19
Charles Hawtrey	17

Teacher (1959)

Kenneth Williams	38
Kenneth Connor	37
Joan Sims	30
Charles Hawtrey	29
Hattie Jacques	28

Constable (1959)

Sid James	40
Kenneth Connor	36
Kenneth Williams	35
Charles Hawtrey	26
Hattie Jacques	21
Joan Sims	16

Regardless (1960)

Kenneth Connor	36
Kenneth Williams	32
Sid James	31
Charles Hawtrey	23
Joan Sims	22
Hattie Jacques	5

Cruising (1962)

Kenneth Connor	49
Kenneth Williams	42
Sid James	41

Cabby (1963)

Sid James	59
Hattie Jacques	38
Kenneth Connor	35
Charles Hawtrey	35
Jim Dale	7

Jack (1963)

Charles Hawtrey	38
Kenneth Williams	32
Jim Dale	8

Spying (1964)

Kenneth Williams	53
Charles Hawtrey	41
Barbara Windsor	36
Jim Dale	15

Cleo (1964)

Kenneth Williams	48
Kenneth Connor	40
Sid James	37
Jim Dale	26
Charles Hawtrey	25
Joan Sims	13

Cowboy (1965)

Sid James	46
Jim Dale	33
Kenneth Williams	28
Peter Butterworth	13
Charles Hawtrey	13
Joan Sims	12
Bernard Bresslaw	7

Screaming (1966)

Peter Butterworth	36
Jim Dale	35
Kenneth Williams	25
Joan Sims	10
Bernard Bresslaw	9
Charles Hawtrey	5

Don't Lose Your Head (1966)

Kenneth Williams	49
Sid James	48
Peter Butterworth	43
Jim Dale	34
Joan Sims	32
Charles Hawtrey	24

Follow That Camel (1967)

Jim Dale	32
Kenneth Williams	28
Peter Butterworth	27
Bernard Bresslaw	19
Charles Hawtrey	15
Joan Sims	8

Doctor (1967)

Bernard Bresslaw	29
Hattie Jacques	28
Kenneth Williams	27
Jim Dale	26
Sid James	23
Charles Hawtrey	13
Barbara Windsor	12
Peter Butterworth	11
Joan Sims	10

Up The Khyber (1968)

Terry Scott	31
Peter Butterworth	27
Bernard Bresslaw	26
Kenneth Williams	25
Sid James	25
Charles Hawtrey	25
Joan Sims	19

Camping (1968)

Sid James	35
Bernard Bresslaw	35
Kenneth Williams	30
Barbara Windsor	28
Terry Scott	24
Joan Sims	23
Hattie Jacques	22
Charles Hawtrey	16
Peter Butterworth	9

Again Doctor (1969)

Jim Dale	65
Kenneth Williams	38
Charles Hawtrey	36
Hattie Jacques	28
Sid James	26
Joan Sims	20
Barbara Windsor	16
Patsy Rowlands	12
Peter Butterworth	2

Up The Jungle (1969)

Sid James	47

Loving (1970)

Sid James	39

Kenneth Connor	35	Hattie Jacques	31
Joan Sims	32	Joan Sims	18
Bernard Bresslaw	23	Bernard Bresslaw	15
Terry Scott	22	Kenneth Williams	14
Charles Hawtrey	9	Terry Scott	14
		Charles Hawtrey	12
		Patsy Rowlands	7
		Peter Butterworth	1

Henry (1970)		*At Your Convenience* (1971)	
Sid James	65	Sid James	48
Kenneth Williams	38	Bernard Bresslaw	37
Joan Sims	32	Kenneth Williams	33
Terry Scott	31	Joan Sims	32
Charles Hawtrey	22	Patsy Rowlands	23
Barbara Windsor	16	Charles Hawtrey	20
Kenneth Connor	14	Hattie Jacques	11
Peter Butterworth	2		
Patsy Rowlands	2		

Matron (1971)		*Abroad* (1972)	
Sid James	44	Sid James	50
Hattie Jacques	42	Kenneth Williams	40
Kenneth Williams	29	Peter Butterworth	38
Terry Scott	23	Joan Sims	37
Bernard Bresslaw	22	Kenneth Connor	36
Kenneth Connor	16	Barbara Windsor	32
Barbara Windsor	12	Charles Hawtrey	28
Charles Hawtrey	9	Bernard Bresslaw	23
Joan Sims	7	Hattie Jacques	13
Patsy Rowlands	3	Jack Douglas	5
Jack Douglas	1	Patsy Rowlands	2

Girls (1973)		*Dick* (1974)	
Sid James	46	Sid James	58
Bernard Bresslaw	34	Kenneth Williams	44
Joan Sims	26	Jack Douglas	42
Barbara Windsor	25	Barbara Windsor	35
Kenneth Connor	22	Bernard Bresslaw	30
Peter Butterworth	21	Peter Butterworth	27
Jack Douglas	19	Kenneth Connor	19

Patsy Rowlands	14	Joan Sims	18
		Hattie Jacques	16
		Patsy Rowlands	1

Behind (1975)

Kenneth Williams	40
Jack Douglas	34
Bernard Bresslaw	28
Kenneth Connor	27
Peter Butterworth	25
Patsy Rowlands	22
Joan Sims	20

England (1976)

Kenneth Connor	63
Jack Douglas	40
Joan Sims	22
Peter Butterworth	12

Emmannuelle (1978)

Jack Douglas	26
Kenneth Williams	18
Kenneth Connor	16
Joan Sims	13
Peter Butterworth	13

Columbus (1992)

Jim Dale	61
Jack Douglas	8

Behind every great actor is a great woman – in this case there are two! Val James, widow of Sid James (left), taken at Carry on Screaming *5th November 2000, and Sue James, his daughter (right). Sue was a consultant for the documentary The* Unforgettable Sid James. *The photo was taken at* Carry On Celebrating *on 29th April 2001*

CARRY ON MEMORY

"I was only in *Carry On Henry*, my main memories are of the waiting times between filming the scenes at Pinewood Studios, when I was often regaled with ultra enthusiastic eulogies on his beliefs about everything, from Kenneth Williams on one side of me, while Terry Scott told me jokes in between reading the *Daily Mirror*, seated on the other side of me! The contrasting approaches in their work and in life gave me great amusement. I'd worked with Sid James previously in his television series and felt a great affection for him. All the cast were friendly and I enjoyed being in the film."

Marjie Lawerence

Total number of Scenes the Stars appeared in the films

Name	Scenes	Average per Film
Sid James	808	42.5
Kenneth Connor	589	34.6
Kenneth Williams	838	33.5
Jim Dale	338	30.7
Bernard Bresslaw	337	24.1
Barbara Windsor	212	23.6
Hattie Jacques	311	22.2
Charles Hawtrey	505	21.9
Jack Douglas	175	21.8
Terry Scott	147	21.0
Joan Sims	495	20.6
Peter Butterworth	307	19.2
Patsy Rowlands	86	9.6

CARRY ON MEMORY

"I played a very, very minor character in two of the films. *Carry On Sergeant* saw me as a glorified extra – part of the platoon. I went straight into the army after that – National Service! Funnily enough the person this Walworth working-class boy got on really well with was James Villiers, also another glorified extra at this time. My first film straight OUT of the army was *Carry On Cabby* I think I mouthed one line, 'you bastard', and got to drive an FX2 taxi! My stepfather was the late Freddie Mills who also featured in two Carry On films *Constable* and *Regardless*".

Don McCorkindale

Billing Running Orders

Sid James	1,1,1,1,1,1,1,3,1,1,1,2,1,1,1,1,1,1,1.	22
Kenneth Williams	8,4,5,5,4,2,1,1,2,2,2,2,4,2,2,2,3,2,2,2,2,2,1,1.	65
Charles Hawtrey	7,3,3,4,3,3,4,3,3,4,4,4,5,4,3,4,4,3,3,3,3,3,3.	83
Kenneth Connor	6,2,2,3,2,3,4,4,5,7,8,6,4,8,4,1,3.	72
Jim Dale	9,7,5,6,3,3,3,2,5,2,1.	46
Joan Sims	9,7,7,5,5,5,5,5,6,10,5,3,5,4,5,4,5,5,4,3,6,5,10,5.	133
Barbara Windsor	2,9,6,6,6,7,9,2,3.	50
Bernard Bresslaw	7,8,8,8,6,7,6,6,6,6,8,5,5,3.	89
Hattie Jacques	13,5,6,8,11,2,6,8,7,4,4,4,7,4.	89
Peter Butterworth	6,7,6,3,7,7,9,9,12,10,5,6,7,8,9,6.	117
Terry Scott	33,8,5,7,7,5,9.	74
Jack Douglas	26,20,8,9,7,5,4,17.	96
Patsy Rowlands	8,11,25,10,13,18,9,10,12.	116

The rear of the Mansion House at Pinewood Studios. The scene was used in Carry On Nurse in 1958, released in 1959

Carry On League of Top Billings

1.	Sid James	1.2
2.	Kenneth Williams	2.6
3.	Charles Hawtrey	3.6
4.	Kenneth Connor	4.2
	Jim Dale	4.2
5.	Joan Sims	5.5
6.	Barbara Windsor	5.6
7.	Bernard Bresslaw	6.4
	Hattie Jacques	6.4
8.	Peter Butterworth	7.3
9.	Terry Scott	10.6
10.	Jack Douglas	12.0
11.	Patsy Rowlands	12.8

CARRY ON MEMORIES

"I was only in two Carry On films which were *Loving* and *Girls*. I cannot remember much about filming the Carry Ons, it's only when people say that they've seen me in a Carry On the other night that I remember I did them, it was just another job. Everyone was very professional. There was a low budget on them and you just had to get on as quickly as you could so that the finished product would come in on time."

Bill Pertwee

* * * * * * * * * *

"I was young and foolish. I never did it again! I was paid £25 a day. The cream fight was fun. The cream was real, so was the stench."

Mike Grady

Carry On Films
The People Behind the Scenes

Have you ever thought about those people whose faces were never seen and how many Carry On films they worked on? Now you know...

Job Description	Name	Number of Films	% Worked On
Producer	Peter Rogers	31	100%
Director	Gerald Thomas	31	100%
Screenplay	Talbot Rothwell	21	67.7%
	Norman Hudis	7	22.6%
	Dave Freeman	3	9.6%
	Sid Colin	2	6.5%
	Dave Pursall	1	3.2%
	Jack Seddon	1	3.2%
	Tony Church	1	3.2%
	Lance Peters	1	3.2%
Music	Eric Rogers	23	74.2%
	Bruce Montgomery	6	19.4%
	Douglas Gamley	1	3.2%
	Max Harris	1	3.2%
	John Du Prez	1	3.2%
Director of Photography	Alan Hume	16	51.6%
	Ernest Steward	10	32.3%
	Reginald Wyer	2	6.5%
	Peter Hennessy	1	3.2%
	Ted Scaife	1	3.2%
	Tony Imi	1	3.2%
Camera Operator	Godrey Godar	9	29.0%
	James Balden	9	29.0%
	Alan Hume	4	12.9%
	Jimmy Devis	4	12.9%
	Dudley Lovell	2	6.5%
	Alan Hall	1	3.2%
	Derek Browne	1	3.2%
	Neil Binney	1	3.2%

Job Description	Name	Number of Films	% Worked On
	Martin Hume	1	3.2%
Art Director	Lionel Couch	11	35.5%
	Alex Vetchinsky	6	19.4%
	Bert Davey	3	9.6%
	Carmen Dillon	2	6.5%
	Jack Stephens	2	6.5%
	Jack Shampan	2	6.5%
	Cedric Dawe	1	3.2%
	John Blezard	1	3.2%
	Robert Jones	1	3.2%
	Peter Childs	1	3.2%
Assistant Director	Jack Causey	7	22.6%
	David Bracknell	6	19.4%
	Peter Bolton	5	16.1%
	Bert Batt	2	6.5%
Production Manager	Jack Swinburne	12	38.7%
	Frank Bevis	9	29.0%
	Roy Goddard	6	19.4%
Editor	Alfred Roome	15	48.4%
	John Shirley	5	16.1%
	Archie Ludski	4	12.9%
	Rod Keys	3	9.6%
	Peter Boita	2	6.5%
Sound/Dubbing Editor	Chris Lancaster	4	12.9%
	Colin Miller	4	12.9%
	Arthur Rideout	3	9.6%
	Peter Best	3	9.6%
	Patrick Foster	3	9.6%
	Seymour Logie	2	6.5%
	Roger Cherrill	2	6.5%
	Leslie Higgins	2	6.5%
	Wally Nelson	2	6.5%
	Brian Holland	2	6.5%
Make Up	Geoffrey Rodway	23	74.2%
	George Blackler	5	16.1%
	Jim Hydes	2	6.5%

Job Description	Name	Number of Films	% Worked On
	W T Partleton	1	3.2%
	Sarah Monzani	1	3.2%
	Amanda Knight	1	3.2%
Continuity	Penny Daniels	6	19.4%
	Joy Mercer	4	12.9%
	Marjorie Lavelly	4	12.9%
	Rita Davidson	3	9.6%
	Joan Davies	2	6.5%
	Gladys Goldsmith	2	6.5%
	Josephine Knowles	2	6.5%
	Susannha Merry	1	3.2%
	Doreen Dernley	1	3.2%
	Tilly Day	1	3.2%
	Olga Brook	1	3.2%
	Yvonne Richards	1	3.2%
	Jane Buck	1	3.2%
Casting Director	Betty White	6	19.4%
	John Owen	2	6.5%
	Gina Jay	1	3.2%
Hairdressing	Stella Rivers	21	67.7%
	Biddy Chrystal	4	12.9%
	Olga Angelinetta	2	6.5%
	Ann Fordyce	1	3.2%
	Sue Love	1	3.2%
	Sarah Love	1	3.2%
	Pearl Orton	1	3.2%
Costume Designer	Courteanay Elliott	11	35.5%
	Joan Ellacott	5	16.1%
	Yvonne Caffin	4	12.9%
	Emma Selby-Walker	4	12.9%
	Anna Duse	1	3.2%
	Julie Harris	1	3.2%
	Cynthia Tingey	1	3.2%

Audrey Skinner, PA to Peter Rogers. Audrey is one of the main people behind the scenes of the Carry On business.

Carry On Script-Writers

Below is a list of the script-writers of the Carry On films...

1. Talbot Rothwell
   (*Cabby, Jack, Spying*, Cleo, Cowboy, Screaming, Don't Lose Your Head, Follow That Camel, Doctor, Up The Khyber, Camping, Again Doctor, Up The Jungle, Loving, Henry, At Your Convenience, Matron, Abroad, Girls, Dick*)

   20 films

2. Norman Hudis
   (*Sergeant, Nurse, Teacher, Constable, Regardless, Cruising*)

   6 films

3. Dave Freeman
   (*Behind, Columbus*)

   2 films

4. Sid Colin
   (*Spying**)

   1 film

   David Pursael
   (*England+*)

   1 film

   Jack Seddon
   (*England+*)

   1 film

   Tony Church
   (*That's Carry On*)

   1 film

   Lance Peters
   (*Emmannuelle*)

   1 film

key: *+ = co-written

Script Ratios

Number of Carry On films the two main script-writers wrote.

1. Talbot Rothwell	20 films in 12 years	60.0
2. Norman Hudis	6 films in 5 years	83.3

Original script-writer Norman Hudis. He wrote the first 6 films from 1958 to 1962.

The Carry On Team Birthdays

Below is a compiled list of the main Carry On teams birthdays and place of birth. *Now you know!*

Patsy Rowlands	19th January 1934	London
Peter Butterworth	4th February 1919	Bramhall
Hattie Jacques	7th February 1924	Sandgate
Peter Rogers (producer)	20th February 1914	Rochester
Kenneth Williams	22nd February 1926	London
Bernard Bresslaw	25th February 1934	East London
Jack Douglas	26th April 1927	Newcastle
Terry Scott	4th May 1927	Watford
Sid James	6th May 1913	Johannesburg
Joan Sims	9th May 1930	Laindon
Kenneth Connor	6th June 1916	London
Norman Hudis (script-writer)	27th July 1922	London
Barbara Windsor	6th August 1937	Shoreditch
Jim Dale	15th August 1935	Rothwell
Alan Hume (cameraman)	16th October 1924	Putney
Talbot Rothwell (script-writer)	12th November 1916	Bromley
Charles Hawtrey	30th November 1934	Hounslow
Gerald Thomas (director)	10th December 1920	Hull

CARRY ON MEMORIES

"I only appeared briefly in one Carry On film which was *Cabby*. My memory is of a group of Japanese journalists coming on to the set at Pinewood and going absolutely crazy with delight when they spotted Kenneth Williams and Charles Hawtrey (especially Charlie!) – Gerald Thomas virtually had to throw them out before we could resume shooting. Would love to have seen the Carry Ons dubbed into Japanese – AH SO!"

Peter Byrne

CARRY ON MEMORIES

"A lovely memory from *Carry On Nurse* was as a hospital visitor under the eagle eye of Hattie Jacques the matron. I was measuring up my film-husband Brian Oulton in his bed for his woolly jumper which I was knitting for him, much to his embarrassment and giggles! Also in *Carry On Constable* outside the ladies loo on Ealing Broadway asking PC Kenneth Connor for change of a penny – I was dying to go! It was grand working with such a brilliant team."

Hilda Fenemore

****

"The memory which I thought might be quite funny for you was on the film *Carry On Jack*, when I played Captain Hardy for the opening screen credits. They had very cleverly reproduced the famous picture of the death of Nelson, which they cross-faded from the picture to the living image of it. The script I remember was very very funny, as Nelson kept saying, 'Kiss me, Hardy' and I kept saying 'I don't think I'd bother, Sir, I don't think it would be good for you and they won't like it back at the Admiralty' to which Nelson again said, 'Kiss me, Hardy', which I regrettably did. At this point he expired and I then said the line 'I told you it would not be good for you, Sir!' and then the film started. This in itself was very funny, but what made it hilarious was that we all had to be absolutely frozen and still at the beginning of the shot, but because we all knew what was going to be said, everybody got the giggles. We eventually had to do it about 16 times, with a very irate Director saying 'Come along now, pull yourselves together. This is serious. We have got to get this shot in.'"

Anton Rodgers

****

"I only spent one day filming on *Carry On Cleo* and one day on *Up The Khyber*. All I can say is I found Jim Dale absolutely charming and friendly, but Kenneth Williams on *Up The Khyber* totally ignored me all day! I was very young and inexperienced at the time, but it taught me as I became more successful to make sure I was polite and welcoming to the young members of any cast I was in!"

Wanda Ventham

CARRY ON MEMORIES

"*Carry On Girls* was like a continuation of *Bless This House* – exactly the same unit, exactly the same location (Pinewood Studios) and virtually the same cast. It was a warm spring in 1973 and Pinewood once again played host this time, though, apart from the guiding hand of Sid James. I was surrounded by some of the best comic talent in the country: Bernard Bresslaw, Barbara Windsor, Joan Sims, June Whitfield, Kenneth Connor and Jimmy Logan to name a few. Talking of talent, there was also a wealth of crumpet plus the getting closer, Sally Geeson. Richard O'Sullivan would wind his way down to the Studios in the evenings and we would laugh until closing time. On one occasion, posing as film producers we managed to expose the bullshit side of the business by convincing some budding investors to put money into a western to be shot in Finland and that would star Jimmy Clitheroe!
Gerald Thomas was also extremely encouraging and by the end of the film my part of Larry the Photographer had increased somewhat. 'Cor, your bleedin' part is getting bigger and bigger darlin', screamed Barbara Windsor."

Robin Askwith
Extract from *Confessions of Robin Askwith*
Published by Ebury 1999. Used by permission of The Random House Group Limited.

* * * * * * * * * *

"I was in the first Carry On film only. I thought the film was dreadful, one of the black and white films of the last century best forgotten. It was rather boring to be in, only lightened at times by Kenneth Williams and his outrageous anecdotes."

Gerald Campion

* * * * * * * * * *

"During *Carry On Sergeant* I was booked for *Carry On Nurse*. Peter Rogers wanted me to play a crossed-eyed person. After two weeks he said 'I was to be crossed in one eye'. I practised for weeks and finely managed to just cross one eye. On the day we started filming *Nurse* he said 'Forget it Ed, we want you to play a man who is impotent!' Peter's little joke!"

Ed Devereaux

Carry On Stars & Co-Stars
Birth & Death Years

Name	Born	Died	Age
Mario Fabrizi (1)	1925	1963	38
Freddie Mills (2)	1922	1965	43
Jerry Desmonde (1)	1908	1967	58
Howerd Crawford (1)	1914	1969	55
EVH Emmett (N)	1902	1971	69
Cecil Parker (1)	1897	1971	74
Kynaston Reeves (1)	1893	1971	78
Denis Shaw (1)	1921	1971	50
Esma Cannon (4)	1896	1972	76
Cyril Raymond (1)	1897	1973	76
Tony Sagar (6)	1920	1973	53
George Woodbridge (1)	1907	1973	66
Cyril Chamberlain (7)	1909	1974	65
Judith Furse (3)	1912	1974	62
William Hartnell (1)	1908	1975	63
Richard Wattis (1)	1912	1975	62
Martin Boddey (2)	1908	1976	68
Sid James (20)	1913	1976	62
William Mervyn (3)	1912	1976	64
Ted Ray (1)	1906	1977	71
Bruce Montgomery (M)	1921	1978	57
Susan Shaw (1)	1929	1978	49
Peter Butterworth (16)	1919	1979	59
Julian Orchard (4)	1930	1979	49
Sidney Tafler (1)	1916	1979	63
Eric Pohlman (2)	1903	1979	76
Imogen Hassall (1)	1942	1980	38
Renee Houston (3)	1902	1980	78
Hattie Jacques (14)	1924	1980	56
Ambrosine Phillpotts (3)	1912	1980	68
Eric Rogers (M)	1913	1981	67
Talbot Rothwell (SW)	1916	1981	64
John Catrell (1)	1907	1981	73
Harry H Corbett (1)	1925	1982	57
Lucy Griffiths (6)	1919	1982	63
Norman Chappel (2)	1929	1983	54

Frances De Wolff (1)	1913	1984	71
Arnold Ridley (1)	1895	1984	89
Frank Forsyth (7)	1905	1984	79
Derek Francis (5)	1923	1984	61
Wilfred Brambell (1)	1912	1985	73
Gordon Rollings (1)	1927	1985	58
Phil Silvers (1)	1912	1985	72
Dandy Nicholls (1)	1907	1986	79
Irene Handl (2)	1901	1987	85
Harry Locke (3)	1915	1987	72
Sidney Bromley (1)	1919	1987	68
Charles Hawtrey (23)	1914	1988	73
Kenneth Williams (26)	1926	1988	62
Robert Dorning (1)	1913	1989	76
Alan Gifford (1)	1905	1989	84
Eric Barker (4)	1912	1990	78
Jill Ireland (1)	1936	1990	54
Carol White (1)	1943	1991	48
Donald Houston (1)	1923	1991	67
Wilfred Hyde-White (1)	1903	1991	87
Percy Herbert (2)	1920	1992	72
Frankie Howerd (2)	1917	1992	75
Cardew Robinson (1)	1917	1992	74
Bob Todd (1)	1921	1992	71
Brian Oulton (4)	1908	1992	84
Bernard Bresslaw (14)	1934	1993	59
Patrick Cargill (2)	1918	1993	74
Kenneth Connor (17)	1916	1993	77
Victor Maddern (5)	1928	1993	65
Gerald Thomas (D)	1920	1993	72
Roy Castle (1)	1932	1994	62
Fred Griffiths (3)	1912	1994	82
Llewellyn Rees (1)	1900	1994	94
Terry Scott (7)	1927	1994	67
Noel Dyson (2)	1916	1995	79
Dany Robin (1)	1927	1995	68
Harold Berens (1)	1903	1995	92
Peter Grant (1)	1935	1995	60
Jon Pertwee (4)	1919	1996	76
Beryl Reid (1)	1920	1996	76

Patrick Cargill (2)	1918	1996	78
Alfred Roome (E)	1907	1997	90
Michael Ward (5)	1909	1997	88
Michael Balfour (1)	1917	1997	80
Don Henderson (1)	1931	1997	66
Patricia Hayes (1)	1909	1998	88
Joan Hickson (5)	1906	1998	92
Davy Kaye (2)	1928	1998	70
James Villiers (1)	1933	1998	65
Betty Marsden (2)	1919	1998	78
Norman Rossington (3)	1928	1999	70
Bill Owen (4)	1914	1999	85
Derek Guyler (1)	1914	1999	85
Peter Jones (2)	1920	2000	79
Brian Rowlinson (3)	1932	2000	68
Norman Mitchell (5)	1919	2001	82
Jimmy Logan (2)	1928	2001	73
Joan Sims (24)	1930	2001	71
Stanley Unwin (1)	1911	2002	90
Pat Coombs (2)	1927	2002	75

Key = (D) Director (P) Producer (SW) Script-Writer (M) Music (C) Cameraman (E) Editor (PH) Photography (N) Narrator ( ) All others are Actors & Actresses with the number of films they appeared in.

CARRY ON MEMORIES

"One day after lunch on the set of *Carry On Nurse* Charles Hawtrey (who enjoyed a drink or two) tripped over an electric cable and fell on top of Peter Rogers, the Producer. Rogers glared up at him from the floor and said 'Pissed', Hawtrey smiled benignly from this position astride the producer and replied 'So am I!' "

Patrick Durkin

****

"I have only appeared in one Carry On, *Carry On Cruising* in which I played the ships drunk. It was a pleasure to work with Esma Cannon, Liz Fraser and Dilys Laye."

Ronnie Stevens

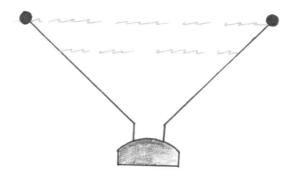

Chapter 3
Television

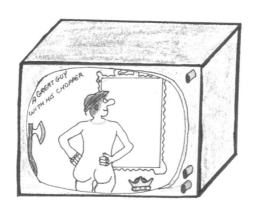

On The Box

The Carry On television programme series started production in 1969 and went on to run for twenty years, peaking in 1975 with 65% of the twenty programmes being televised in this year. All twenty programmes were produced between October and February. Although a spin off from the now famous Carry On films, they never quite reached the pinnacle of success the films acquired, but still were written, produced and directed in the humorous Carry On fashion, and done extremely well.

The television productions used eleven of the main Carry On team, Kenneth Connor making eighteen appearances out of the twenty productions, a staggering 90%. The other Kenneth (Williams) never appeared in a single television programme. The only other regular team member not to appear was Jim Dale. Jack Douglas appeared in thirteen programmes in a row without missing one, some 76.5% of all seventeen he made. As in both the films and stage shows, Sid James again topped the billing orders.

A new script writer Dave Freeman wrote almost half of the Carry On programme for television and then went on to write two Carry On films, *Behind* (1975) and *Columbus* (1992).

"Get Away!"

Number one of the Carry Ons
and rightly so. Peter Rogers
producer, taken 15th December 2002

Carry On Television Programmes Broadcasted

Title	Month	Year	Length	Stars	Colour/bw
Christmas	Dec	1969	50 mins	8	Colour
Again Christmas	Dec	1970	50 mins	8	b/w
Christmas	Dec	1972	50 mins	11	Colour
What A Carry On	Oct	1973	50 mins	6	Colour
Christmas	Dec	1973	50 mins	9	Colour
The Prisoner Of Spenda	Jan	1975	21 mins	10	Colour
The Baron Outlook	Jan	1975	24 mins	12	Colour
The Sobbing Cavalier	Jan	1975	23 mins	8	Colour
Orgy And Bess	Jan	1975	23 mins	10	Colour
One In The Eye For Harold	Feb	1975	24 mins	14	Colour
The Nine Old Cobblers	Feb	1975	24 mins	9	Colour
The Case Of The Screaming Winkles	Nov	1975	24 mins	11	Colour
The Case Of The Coughing Parrot	Nov	1975	24 mins	10	Colour
Under The Round Table	Oct	1975	25 mins	14	Colour
Short Knights, Long Daze	Nov	1975	24 mins	11	Colour
And In My Lady's Chamber	Nov	1975	25 mins	10	Colour
Who Needs Kitchener?	Nov	1975	25 mins	10	Colour
Lamp-Posts Of The Empire	Dec	1975	24 mins	11	Colour
Christmas Classics	Dec	1983	24 mins	25	Colour
Norbert Smith – A Life	Nov	1989	52 mins	14	Colour

CARRY ON MEMORY

"I only did one Carry On film – *Carry On Regardless* and I only worked on it for four days, so I'm afraid I have no cheerful reflections, although everyone was very nice and poor old Freddie Mills was charming."

Terence Alexander

Television Programmes Made

Years	Number	%	Months	Number	%
1975	13	65%	November	6	30%
1973	2	10%	December	6	30%
1969	1	5%	January	4	20%
1970	1	5%	February	2	10%
1972	1	5%	October	2	10%
1983	1	5%			
1989	1	5%			

Averages

Stars 221 = 11 in each programme.

Running time total 636 minutes = Average of 31.8 minutes per show

95% filmed in colour   5% filmed in b/w

CARRY ON MEMORY

"My memories of 'Carry On' are very misty and obscure. I did two of the films *Loving* and *At Your Convenience* – small contributions amounting to about 2/3 days in total. I do remember a scene with Kenneth Williams who was very easy to work with – amusing, but I thought underneath rather sad. He seemed strangely not happy about what he was working on, a nice man but... That's the only thing I took away from it all. All this took place in the early '70s not surprising it's a bit misty!"

Philip Stone

Carry On Television Appearances

Listed below is a league of the top twelve television appearances by the stars.

		Number	*Percentage*
1.	Kenneth Connor	18	90%
2.	Jack Douglas	17	85%
3.	Barbara Windsor	15	75%
4.	Peter Butterworth	14	70%
	Joan Sims		
5.	Bernard Bresslaw	9	45%
	Sid James		
6.	Brian Osborne	8	40%
7.	Norman Chappell	7	35%
	David Lodge		
8.	John Carlin	6	30%
9.	Sherrie Hewson	5	25%
10.	Billy Cornelius	4	20%
	Hattie Jacques		
11.	Carol Hawkins	3	15%
	Charles Hawtrey		
	Vivienne Johnson		
	Diane Langton		
	Victor Maddern		
	Terry Scott		
12.	Brian Capron	2	10%
	Julian Holloway		
	Linda Hooks		
	Frankie Howerd		
	Oscar James		
	Valerie Leon		
	Desmond Mcnamara		
	Michael Nightingale		
	Andrew Ray		
	Patsy Rowlands		
	Ronnie Brody		

Also other stars like Johnny Briggs, Harry Enfield, Laraine Humphreys, Marianne Stone and Melvyn Hayes made appearances in Carry On TV who also had an association with the films.

Sustained Appearances in Carry On Television

These are the top six sustained appearances in the Carry On television series by the stars without missing a programme. (Compiled from 1969 to 1989).

1. Jack Douglas   13   65%
   (from The Sobbing Cavalier to Norbert Smith – A Life)

2. Kenneth Connor   12   60%
   (from Orgy And Bess to Norbert Smith – A Life)

3. Barbara Windsor   9   45%
   (from Christmas '69 to Orgy And Bess)

4. Joan Sims   8   40%
   (from One In The Eye For Harold to Who Needs Kitchener?)

5. Bernard Bresslaw   6   30%
   (from Under The Round Table to Laughing Christmas Classics)
   Peter Butterworth
   (from Christmas '72 to the Sobbing Cavalier)
   Sid James
   (from What A Carry On to Orgy And Bess)

6. John Carlin   4   20%
   (from Orgy And Bess to The Case Of The Screaming Winkles)
   Norman Chappell
   (from The Case Of The Screaming Winkles to Short Knight, Long Daze)
   David Lodge
   (from One In The Eye For Harold to The Case Of The Laughing Parrot)
   Brian Osborne
   (from The Baron Outlook to One In The Eye For Harold)

Carry On Television
League of Billing Orders

1.	Sid James	1.0		7.	Jack Douglas	3.6
2.	Terry Scott	2.0		8.	Peter Butterworth	4.5
3.	Hattie Jacques	2.3		9.	Bernard Bresslaw	5.0
4.	Kenneth Connor	2.6		10.	Patsy Rowlands	7.0
5.	Barbara Windsor	2.9		11.	Frankie Howerd	8.0
6.	Charles Hawtrey	3.0				
	Joan Sims	3.0				

* Does not include *Carry On Christmas* classics as appeared in alphabetical
  order in the billing.

CARRY ON MEMORY

"Up until the day I agreed to do the first Carry On I had been a serious
stuntman and thought that films such as Carry On were a joke, but I
found out that although the money was tight they expected the best. I had
some great times making these cut-price movies, made all the better by
getting to know some wonderful people like Dora Bryan, Bill Owen, Sid
James (who was the best tapper in the business), Joan Sims, who I used to
drop off home on many occasions as it was on my way, and Phil Silvers
who on screen was one of my favourites. Not a lot of people know this,
but at the time of my first Carry On I had been dabbling in a bit of
theatre work in such plays as *Mr Roberts* with Tyrone Power and *Wish You
Were Here* and there were a lot of muscle guys which attended the
audition for Carry On, among them Sean Connery, who was a top
Mr Universe contestant at the time."

Nosher Powell

Carry On Television
Billing Orders

Sid James	1,1,1,1,1,1,1,1	8
Terry Scott	2,2	4
Charles Hawtrey	3,3	6
Hattie Jacques	4,1,2	7
Barbara Windsor	5,5,3,2,3,2,3,3,4,3,2,2,1,3	41
Bernard Bresslaw	6,6,5,4,4,6,5,4	40
Peter Butterworth	7,5,4,5,3,4,5,4,6,3,3,5,5	59
Frankie Howerd	8	8
Kenneth Connor	4,4,3,4,5,3,2,2,2,2,1,1,1,1	41
Joan Sims	2,2,4,2,4,3,4,3,3,2,2,4,4	39
Jack Douglas	7,6,7,6,2,5,1,1,1,1,5,5,3,3,3,2	58
Patsy Rowlands	7	7

* Does not include *Carry On Christmas* classics as appeared in alphabetical order in the billing.

Carry On Television Writers
The league of television scriptwriters.

	Name	Number Written	Percentage
1.	Dave Freeman	9	45%
	(Again Christmas+, Christmas*, Prisoner Of Spenda, Baron Outlook, Sobbing Cavalier, Nine Old Cobblers, Case Of The Screaming Winkles, Case Of The Coughing Parrot, Christmas Classics#)		
2.	Lew Scharz	6	30%
	(One In The Eye For Harold, Under The Round Table, Short Knight, Long Daze, And In My Lady's Chamber, Who Needs Kitchener?, Lamp-posts Of The Empire)		
3.	Talbot Rothwell	4	20%
	(Christmas, Christmas, Christmas, Christmas Classics#)		
4.	Sid Colin	1	5%
	(Again Christmas+)		
	Barry Cryer	1	5%
	(Orgy and Bess>)		
	Dick Vosburgh	1	5%
	(Orgy And Bess>)		
	Harry Enfield	1	5%
	(Norbert Smith – A Life<)		
	Geoff Perkins	1	5%
	(Norbert Smith – A Life<)		

key: + * # > < = co-written.

The People Behind the Scenes

The People who worked behind the scenes on the Carry On television programmes are listed below.

Title	Number worked on	Percentage
Graphics		
George Wallder	13	65%
Animator		
Len Lewis	11	55%
Sound		
Len Penfold	7	35%
Cameras		
Mike Whitcutt	7	35%
Make-Up		
Sheila Mann	7	35%
Wardrobe		
James Dark	7	35%
Executive Producer/Producer		
Gerald Thomas	16	80%
Peter Rogers	16	80%
Peter Eton	2	10%
Geoffrey Perkins	2	10%
Director		
Allan Tarrant	14	70%
Ronnie Baxter	2	10%
Ronald Fouracre	1	5%
David Clark	1	5%
Geoff Posner	1	5%
Designer		
Richard Lake	3	15%
Roger Allen	2	10%
Ray White	2	10%
Lewis Logan	2	10%
Brian Holgate	2	10%
Anthony Walker	2	10%

Chapter 4
Stage

Treading the Boards

After producing twenty five successful Carry On films and four successful television programmes, the "Rogers and Thomas" partnership tried their luck at carrying on in the theatre. Immediately after finishing *Carry On Girls* on 25th May 1973, Peter Rogers assembled six of his regular team for the stage show *Carry On London*. It was initially performed at The Birmingham Hippodrome between 14th and 29th September 1973. It worked, who would have doubted it, as anything with the Carry On logo attached to it would work anywhere.

So the production moved onto The Victoria Palace, London where it was directed by the late Bill Roberton, brother of Carry On star Jack Douglas. The show ran for almost a year and a half all but a few days. Two more successful shows followed both in the summer seasons of 1975 and 1992, in Scarborough and Blackpool respectively.

It took fifty-two production staff to produce the three Carry On hit stage shows, with also fourteen companies involved in supplying their services.

Carry On showing "ooh matron"

CARRY ON MEMORY

"It was so long ago – over thirty years – that I can only recall the main events that happened. It was my second television since leaving RADA in 1968. I was at the Birmingham Rep: the 'old rep' as it is called now. At that time the Artistic Director was Peter Dews, a wonderful director and a great teacher of young actors. For this particular episode I was to play and sing the links between the various scenes, a sort of wandering minstrel. When the day arrived for filming my 'wandering', it was pouring with rain! So I did most of the scenes leaning nonchalantly in covered doorways or under thick trees. I met Bernard Bresslaw, who I think was directing, and he was very kind and generous to this young actor. On reflection I am glad that I was young when I did it. The thought now of composing and playing the guitar – I had only just begun to learn this instrument – would be pretty daunting. There was such a good atmosphere on the location that one could hardly fail. Wonderful times. I loved the Carry On television and film series. Uncompromisingly English."

Desmond McNamara

Carry On Stage Shows

The three Carry On stage shows that were performed were:

1. *Carry On London* from 4.10.73 to 31.3.75
   (The Victoria Palace, London)   (2 acts – duration 2 hours 30 mins)

The Sketches

Act 1

Round about Victoria!!
What a Carry On!
Carry On Girls
Emergency Ward 99 and a bit
Deauville 1900
Elizabethan Madrigals
London Night Out
Curtain time at the Royal Standard Music Hall

Act 2

Carry On London
Hello Dollies
Be Prepared
Cleopatra's Palace on the Nile
Cleopatra's Boudoir
Smile

2. *Carry On Laughing* with *"The Slimming Factory"* from 16.6.75 to 30.9.75
   (Royal Opera House, Scarborough)   (2 acts – duration 2 hours 35 mins)
   A Play based on the residents of the Get-U-Fit Health Farm

The Sketches

Act 1

Scene 1 Monday Morning
Scene 2 Wednesday Morning

Act 2

Thursday Afternoon
Thursday Night

3. *Wot a Carry On in Blackpool* from 22.5.92 to 25.10.92
   (The North Pier, Blackpool)   (2 acts – duration 2 hours 30 mins)

The Sketches

Act 1

Arrival
Rehearsals
Out of Town just go to the Movies

Act 2

It's Show Time
London Medley
Wot a Carry On

Carry On Stage Appearances

The team league of stage appearances

1. Barbara Windsor   2   66.7%
   (London, Wot A Carry On In Blackpool)

   Kenneth Connor   2   66.7%
   (London, Carry On Laughing With The Slimming Factory)

   Peter Butterworth   2   66.7%
   (London, Carry On Laughing With The Slimming Factory)

   Bernard Bresslaw   2   66.7%
   (London, Wot A Carry On In Blackpool)

   Jack Douglas   2   66.7%
   (London, Carry On Laughing With The Slimming Factory)

2. Sid James   1   33.3%
   (London)

   Liz Fraser   1   33.3%
   (Carry On Laughing With The Slimming Factory)

   Linda Hooks   1   33.3%
   (Carry On Laughing With The Slimming Factory)

   Anne Aston   1   33.3%
   (Carry On Laughing With The Slimming Factory)

Carry On Stage Billing Orders

Sid James	1,	1
Barbara Windsor	2,2,	4
Kenneth Connor	3,2,	5
Peter Butterworth	4,3,	7
Bernard Bresslaw	5,1,	6
Jack Douglas	6,1,	7
Liz Fraser	4,	4

Carry On Stage
League of Billing Orders

As in both the films and television billings Sid James again comes out on top in the stage billings. He was in no doubt the anchorman in the entire Carry On series. When appearing in *Carry On London* at the Victoria Palace, Sid, with fellow teams members Barbara Windsor, Kenneth Connor, Bernard Bresslaw, Peter Butterworth and Jack Douglas were also making *Carry On Dick* in March and April of 1974, what dedication to the Carry Ons!

1.	Sid James	1.0
2.	Barbara Windsor	2.0
3.	Kenneth Connor	2.5
4.	Bernard Bresslaw	3.0
5.	Peter Butterworth	3.5
	Jack Douglas	3.5
6.	Liz Fraser	4.0

Jack Douglas

Jack entered the team very late, in fact in 1971, with a small role in Matron *and stayed until* Colombus*. He was instantly accepted by all fellow members, and went on to star in a number of Carry On television specials and two Carry On stage shows. Jack is one of only a few to star in film, television and stage versions of the Carry Ons.*

CARRY ON MEMORY

Carry On London – "It was a great thrill to be on stage live with the team and we had a wonderful time. I worked mostly with Sid James and we were great mates. During rehearsals he said to me 'Don't ad-lib with me on stage because I can't ad-lib', but he said, 'You will always get my lines the same every night and if there are any ad-libs to be done, you do them', it was a wonderful relationship, which we both enjoyed. We opened at the Birmingham Hippodrome and then went into the Victoria Palace where we were packed for eighteen months."

Jack Douglas

Carry On Stage Writers

Name	Number Written	Percentage
1. Sam Cree	1	100%
(Carry On Laughing With The Slimming Factory)		
2= Barry Cryer	1*	50%
(Wot A Carry On In Blackpool)		
Dick Vosburgh	1*	50%
(Wot A Carry On In Blackpool)		
3= Talbot Rothwell	1#	33.3%
(London)		
Dave Freeman	1#	33.3%
(London)		
Eric Merriman	1#	33.3%
(London)		

key: #* = co-written

Only two Carry On scriptwriters were involved in film, television and stage productions. They were Talbot Rothwell and Dave Freeman who between them had written thirty seven out of fifty four productions, amounting to 68.5% of all Carry Ons. With original film scriptwriter Norman Hudis, the figure raises to an astonishing 79.6% – well that's a hell of a lot of writing!

The Big Three Scriptwriters

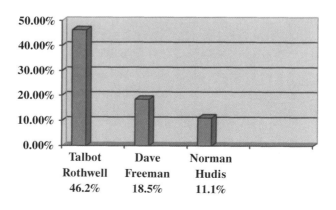

Talbot Rothwell	Dave Freeman	Norman Hudis
46.2%	18.5%	11.1%

Stage Shows
The People Behind the Scenes

Job Description	Number Worked On	Percentage
Director		
Bill Roberton	2	66.7%
Tudor Davies	1	33.3%
Stage Director/Manager		
Alan West	1	33.3%
Tommy Layton	1	33.3%
Sharon Curtis	1	33.3%
Manager		
Alan West	1	33.3%
John Palmer	1	33.3%
Peter Waters	1	33.3%
Designer		
Tod Kingman	1	33.3%
Saxon Lucas	1	33.3%
Gareth Bowen	1	33.3%
Wardrobe		
Eve Barnes	1	33.3%
Judi Kingman	1	33.3%
Heidi Wynter	1	33.3%
Choreography		
Tommy Shaw	1	50.0%
Paul Robinson	1	50.0%

Chapter 5
Overall

The Ballroom which ajoins the theatre –
Pinewood Studios. Final Scene used in Carry
On Loving *(1970), and the Carry On*
Conventions

What! All That!

Undoubtedly the most famous name to us, the general public, was the loveable Sid James – also known as the anchorman within the Carry On team. He holds the record for top billing in the Carry On films, television and stage productions.

"Cor Blimey!"

In 1971 a new member joined the Carry On team by the name of Jack Douglas. He was instantly accepted by all former members. Jack ranks at number five in the overall list of appearances, with an astonishing twenty-eight to his credit, quite a feat for someone joining the team fourteen years into the series.

"wuhey give over!"

Kenneth Williams holds the record with twenty-six appearances out of thirty-one films. The top female performer in the films was Joan Sims with twenty-four to her credit. She also holds the record for sustained appearances with twenty-one films on the trot. Charles Hawtrey made the most number of films in the least number of years, twenty-three films in fifteen years.

Kenneth Connor tops the television appearances with eighteen, a staggering 90% of programmes produced.

"ooh matron!"

Outside of the Mansion House in Pinewood Studios, scene used in Carry On Again Doctor *(1969)*

Carry-Ons Made

The total of all the Carry Ons ever made.

Films	31	57.4%
Television Shows	20	37.0%
Stage Shows	3	5.6%
Total	54	100.0%

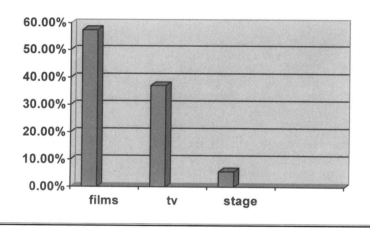

The Big Three
Overall Script-Writers

1.	Talbot Rothwell	20,4,1	8.3
2.	Dave Freeman	2,9,1	4.0
3.	Norman Hudis	6,0,0	2.0

Overall Carry On Appearances
For Films, TV and Stage

1. Joan Sims	38	70.4%
2. Kenneth Connor	37	68.5%
3. Peter Butterworth	32	59.3%
4. Sid James	29	53.7%
5. Jack Douglas	28	51.9%
6. Kenneth Williams Barbara Windsor	27	50.0%
7. Charles Hawtrey	26	48.1%
8. Bernard Bresslaw	25	46.3%
9. Hattie Jacques	18	33.3%
10. Michael Nightingale	12	22.2%
11. Jim Dale Patsy Rowlands	11	20.4%
12. Julian Holloway Terry Scott Peter Gilmore	10	18.5%
13. Marianne Stone	9	16.6%
14. Valerie Leon	8	14.8%

In the Carry On films Charles Hawtrey ranks third – if it wasn't for arguments over his billing order with producer Peter Rogers he would have been top of the league, as other stars such as Kenneth Williams and Joan Sims were contracted to other work, which left them out of various Carry On films. Why argue over the billing orders when you could have topped the Carry On star league? A lot of people would have given their right arm to head such a list of celebrities in the best comedy film series in the world, but instead the honour went to Kenneth Williams.

Overall Billing Running Orders

Listed below are the overall billing running orders for the Carry On films, television and stage productions.

1.	Sid James	1,1,1	1.0
2.	Kenneth Williams	2,0,0	2.0
3.	Kenneth Connor	4,4,3	3.6
4.	Jim Dale	4,0,0	4.0
5.	Barbara Windsor	6,5,2	4.3
6.	Charles Hawtrey	3,6,0	4.5
7.	Hattie Jacques	7,3,0	5.0
8.	Joan Sims	5,6,0	5.5
	Terry Scott	9,2,0	5.5
9.	Bernard Bresslaw	7,9,4	6.6
10.	Peter Butterworth	8,8,5	7.0
11.	Jack Douglas	10,7,5	7.3
12.	Patsy Rowlands	11,10,0	10.5

Carry On Films Released by:

1. Rank Organisation   17   54.8%
    (from *Don't Lose Your Head* to *That's Carry On*, films 13 to 29)

2. Anglo Amalgamated   12   38.7%
    (from *Sergeant* to *Screaming*, films 1 to 12)

3. Hemdale   1   3.2%
    (*Emmannuelle*, film 30)
    Island World   1   3.2%
    (*Columbus*, film 31)

Carry On TV Programmes Production by:

1. ATV Network   14   70%
    (*Wot a Carry On*, programme 4, from *The Prisoner of Spenda* to
    Lamp-Posts of the Empire, programmes 6 to 18)

2. Thames   5   25%
    (from *Christmas 1969* to *Christmas 1972*, programmes 1 to 3
    Christmas 1973, programme 5 and *Christmas Classics*, programme 19)

3. Channel 4   1   5%
    (*Norbert Smith – A Life*, programme 20)

Carry On Stage Shows Presented by:

1. Louis Benjamin   1   33.3%
    (*The Peter Rogers Production*)
    (*Carry On London*)
    Don Robinson   1   33.3%
    (in association with Peter Rogers and Gerald Thomas)
    (*Carry On Laughing with The Slimming Factory*)
    Mike Hughes   1   33.3%
    (Liver Productions Ltd)
    (*Wot a Carry On in Blackpool*)

Chapter 6
The Production
(films)

Inside Pinewood Studios

A Peep Behind the Scenes

While you sit watching the hilarious Carry On films, has it ever crossed your mind what went into producing one of the films? In this chapter of the book we look at some interesting statistics and technical data from the films, which enable you the fan to get an insight into those elusive production notes, which have been held at the British Film Institute, London, since 1992. After the completion of the final film in the series, which was *Carry On Columbus*, Gerald Thomas (director) sent all of the production notes from all thirty films from Pinewood Studios to the Institute where they are stored for future authors to use as a research source for information to put into new Carry On books like this edition.

The boxes contain interesting correspondence from the stars and also contracts from Adder Productions, who dealt with the financial agreements. For every box of production papers there is also a box of original scripts to the films. What follows makes very interesting reading for the fan.

"I only arsked!"

Sir Donald Sinden CBE unveiling a plaque to celebrate Peter Rogers' 50 years in the film business at Pinewood Studios, on the 29th April 2001

Filming the Carry Ons

The shooting schedule on the Carry Ons was always the same, six five-day weeks, eight and a half hours per day, never any overtime.

The camera equipment was basic, one 35mm NC Mitchell camera with six lenses, ranging from 18 mm to 75 mm, plus zoom lens 20 mm to 200 mm. The usual tripods and heads for panning and tilting the camera, also what is called a "dolly" – for tracking the camera around as and when required. We would also use a small hand-held camera for picking up odd close-ups and action shots. The usual shooting procedure was as follows:

Gerald Thomas would walk the scene through with the actors on set, so that the camera and sound crew could mark the floor for the actor's positions, also the relevant camera positions. When this was done Gerald would usually sit with the actors and rehearse the dialogue.

Whilst this was happening, the camera and lighting crew would get the shot set-up and lit. We would average around twenty set-ups per day, very seldom doing more than two to three takes. Sometimes we would need to shoot more takes, almost always due to the actors creating convulsive laughter both in front and behind the camera. It was always great fun working on a Carry On movie and it was a real pleasure to be at work.

The films were always tightly scheduled, efficiently prepared and organized by their producer Peter Rogers.

Gerald was an expert editor and knew exactly what he wanted to shoot in the way of long shots, medium shots and close-ups, always giving himself plenty of options for finally editing each scene. His great competence as a director was responsible for there being a happy atmosphere on the shooting set. I have nothing but happy memories of the time I spent while shooting sixteen Carry On films.

Alan Hume

Alan Hume
Cameraman & Director of Photography

Pinewood Studios
The Stages used in the production of the Carry On Films

Eight different stages were used in the production of the thirty Carry On films. While researching some notes I came across a list of these and their sizes to give the fan an idea of the space required making a set for a scene in the films.

Large Stages

A	165 feet x 110 feet	18,150 square feet
D	165 feet x 110 feet	18,150 square feet
E	165 feet x 110 feet	18,150 square feet

Medium Stages

B	110 feet x 82 feet	9,020 square feet
C	110 feet x 82 feet	9,020 square feet

Small Stages

F	54 feet x 50 feet	2,700 square feet
G	57 feet x 80 feet	4,560 square feet
H	57 feet x 57 feet	3,249 square feet

Inside of Sound Stage D one of the largest stages used in the making of the Carry On Films

The Orchard at Pinewood Studios, scene used in Carry On Camping *(1968),* Carry On Behind *(1975) and* Carry On England *(1976)*

The Church in Denham village, used for the final scene in Carry On Matron, *shot on 2nd November 1971 and released in 1972*

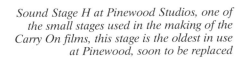

Sound Stage H at Pinewood Studios, one of the small stages used in the making of the Carry On films, this stage is the oldest in use at Pinewood, soon to be replaced

CARRY ON SERGEANT - 1958

The first film of the series, featured William Hartnell, who later went on to *Doctor Who* fame in the '60s, as Sgt Major Grinshaw. Set in the army barracks of Heathercrest Service Depot, a group of recruits join up to serve their country in national service to come up with a champion platoon, – very able! Besides Hartnell, this was also Bob Monkhouse and Dora Bryan's only appearance in a Carry On film.

Data
Film: B&W
Format: Feature Film
Standard Projection: 24 fps
Running Time: 1 hr 23 mins
Gauge: 35 mm
Aspect Ratio: 1.75
Certificate: U
Reels: 10

You squirt!

Production Staff
Male: 16
Female: 4

Film Started: March 1958
Film Finished: May 1958
Film Released: August 1958
Locations Used: 3

Main Team Billings
1. Kenneth Connor
2. Charles Hawtrey
3. Kenneth Williams
4. Hattie Jacques
5. Terry Scott

Charlie Sage and Peter Golightly had to get fire extinguishers ready for inspection – and you can guess what happened to Captain Potts!

CARRY ON NURSE - 1958

The fist medical drama of the Carry Ons. Set on a ward, the story follows a selection of patients through their stay in hospital, being cared for by the delightful Shirley Eaton, in the second of her three Carry On films. This film includes the hilarious laughing gas scene when trying to operate on Leslie Phillips' bunion, also with the gambling colonel betting on is horses and wondering if they ever come in (and he did) finally ending with the now famous daffodil joke in Wilfred Hyde-Whites bottom. Over 2,000,000 plastic daffodils were imported from Japan to advertise the film. Well, it certainly did the trick, with *Nurse* being a cult film on the American campuses. Forty-five years on, and the scene is still a classic.

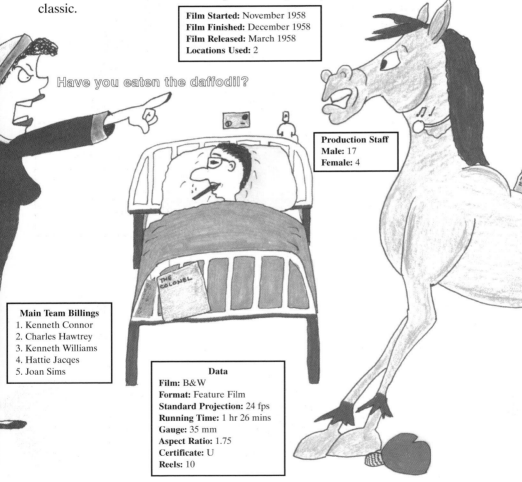

Film Started: November 1958
Film Finished: December 1958
Film Released: March 1958
Locations Used: 2

Have you eaten the daffodil?

Production Staff
Male: 17
Female: 4

Main Team Billings
1. Kenneth Connor
2. Charles Hawtrey
3. Kenneth Williams
4. Hattie Jacqes
5. Joan Sims

Data
Film: B&W
Format: Feature Film
Standard Projection: 24 fps
Running Time: 1 hr 26 mins
Gauge: 35 mm
Aspect Ratio: 1.75
Certificate: U
Reels: 10

CARRY ON TEACHER – 1959

Ted Ray's one and only appearance in a Carry On as Mr Wakefield, the Headmaster of Maudlin Street School. Set around a gang of children intent on giving the school a bad name, thus stopping Mr Wakefield leaving at the end of term. The gang includes a young Richard O'Sullivan who later went on to *Man About the House* and *Robin's Nest* fame in the 1970s. One of the gang's pranks was the sawn-off piano leg. This film sees the Carry on team at their best in the third film of the series.

Ooh, me legs gone!

Production Staff
Male: 13
Female: 4

Film Started: March 1959
Film Finished: April 1959
Film Released: August 1959
Locations Used: 1

Data
Film: B&W
Format: Feature Film
Standard Projection: 24 fps
Running Time: 1 hr 26 mins
Gauge: 35 mm
Aspect Ratio: 1.75
Certificate: U
Reels: 10

Main Team Billings
1. Kenneth Connor
2. Charles Hawtrey
3. Kenneth Williams
4. Hattie Jacqes
5. Joan Sims

107

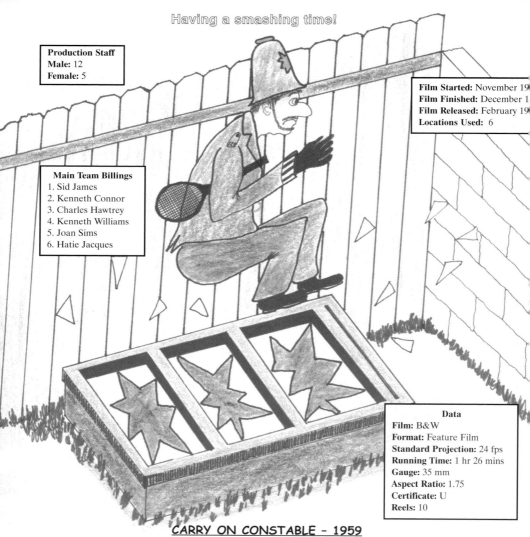

Production Staff
Male: 12
Female: 5

Film Started: November 19
Film Finished: December 1
Film Released: February 19
Locations Used: 6

Main Team Billings
1. Sid James
2. Kenneth Connor
3. Charles Hawtrey
4. Kenneth Williams
5. Joan Sims
6. Hatie Jacques

Data
Film: B&W
Format: Feature Film
Standard Projection: 24 fps
Running Time: 1 hr 26 mins
Gauge: 35 mm
Aspect Ratio: 1.75
Certificate: U
Reels: 10

CARRY ON CONSTABLE – 1959

The fourth film in the series and the introduction of the legend, Sid James, as Sergeant Frank Wilkins (156), in charge of the new recruits from the police training school, which included Leslie Phillips as Constable Tom Potter (129). One of the Hertfordshire Potters, he arrives for duty complete with tennis racquet under his arm. Filmed in Ealing West London and, of course, Pinewood Studios, one of Norman Hudis' finest, bringing out the old cops and robbers chase scene, ending with the recruits victorious, which kept Sergeant Wilkins in his job.

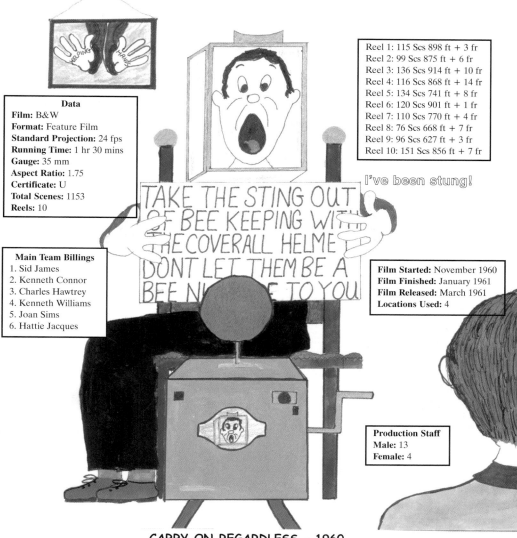

Data
Film: B&W
Format: Feature Film
Standard Projection: 24 fps
Running Time: 1 hr 30 mins
Gauge: 35 mm
Aspect Ratio: 1.75
Certificate: U
Total Scenes: 1153
Reels: 10

Reel 1: 115 Scs 898 ft + 3 fr
Reel 2: 99 Scs 875 ft + 6 fr
Reel 3: 136 Scs 914 ft + 10 fr
Reel 4: 116 Scs 868 ft + 14 fr
Reel 5: 134 Scs 741 ft + 8 fr
Reel 6: 120 Scs 901 ft + 1 fr
Reel 7: 110 Scs 770 ft + 4 fr
Reel 8: 76 Scs 668 ft + 7 fr
Reel 9: 96 Scs 627 ft + 3 fr
Reel 10: 151 Scs 856 ft + 7 fr

I've been stung!

TAKE THE STING OUT OF BEE KEEPING WITH THE COVERALL HELMET DONT LET THEM BE A BEE N... TO YOU

Main Team Billings
1. Sid James
2. Kenneth Connor
3. Charles Hawtrey
4. Kenneth Williams
5. Joan Sims
6. Hattie Jacques

Film Started: November 1960
Film Finished: January 1961
Film Released: March 1961
Locations Used: 4

Production Staff
Male: 13
Female: 4

CARRY ON REGARDLESS – 1960

Based around the Helping Hands agency, headed by Bert Handy (Sid James), this film sees the team up to all sorts of tasks: Kenneth Williams taking Yoki the chimpanzee for a walk and trying to hail a cab, with the cabby saying, "I'll take you, but not your mate!" This line wasn't written by Norman Hudis, but was a great piece of improvisation by the London cabby. Also Kenneth having his photograph taken with a bee protection hat covering his good looks. *Regardess* was Norman's least favourite of the six he had written. It was filmed in Park Street, Windsor, where the same street was used in *Loving* ten years later.

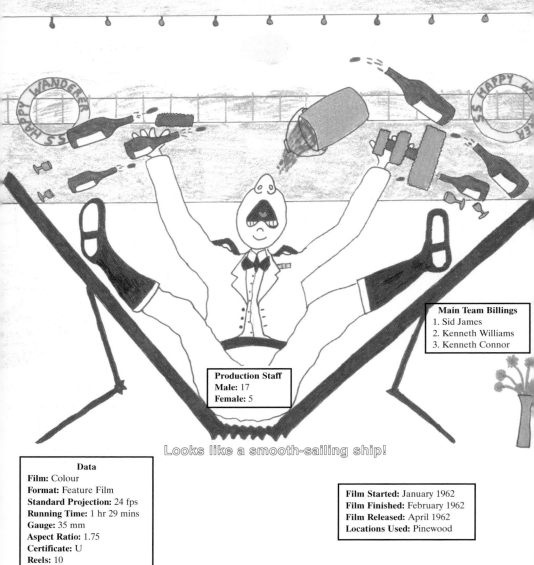

Main Team Billings
1. Sid James
2. Kenneth Williams
3. Kenneth Connor

Production Staff
Male: 17
Female: 5

Looks like a smooth-sailing ship!

Data
Film: Colour
Format: Feature Film
Standard Projection: 24 fps
Running Time: 1 hr 29 mins
Gauge: 35 mm
Aspect Ratio: 1.75
Certificate: U
Reels: 10

Film Started: January 1962
Film Finished: February 1962
Film Released: April 1962
Locations Used: Pinewood

CARRY ON CRUISING - 1962

Cruising was the first film to be filmed in colour. New recruits join the SS
Happy Wanderer as part of Captain Wellington Crowther's well-established
team. In a scene from the film Marjoribanks (Kenneth Williams) thought the
captain had taken to the bottle and wanted to relieve him of command. Totally
filmed on the sound stages at Pinewood Studios, the team were hoping for
sunnier climates, but it wasn't to be.

Production Staff
Male: 18
Female: 3

Main Team Billings
1. Sid James
2. Hattie Jacqes
3. Charles Hawtrey
4. Kenneth Connor
5. Jim Dale

Fancy a lift?

Data
Film: B&W
Format: Feature Film
Standard Projection: 24 fps
Running Time: 1 hr 31 mins
Gauge: 35 mm
Aspect Ratio: 1.75
Certificate: U
Total Scenes Used: 262
Stills Produced: 264
Still Published: 122
Reels: 10

Film Started: March 1963
Film Finished: May 1953
Film Released: June 1958
Locations Used: 5

CARRY ON CABBY - 1963

Cabby saw the first film in the series written by Talbot (Tolly) Rothwell. It reportedly took him just two weeks to come up with the script for this masterpiece. This film also saw the first appearance of Jim Dale, who was recommended by Kenneth Williams, and introduced him into the Carry On fold. He went on to make another nine films. *Cabby* was filmed in and around Windsor. It remains one of the true classics of the ever-popular Carry Ons.

Carry On Cabby (1963)

Listed below is a breakdown of where and how many scenes were shot for this classic.

Date	Pinewood Stage	Number of scenes
25.3.63	C	9
26.3.63	C	2
27.3.63	C	6
28.3.63	lot	4
29.3.63	C	4
1.4.63	lot	7
2.4.63	C & lot	16
3.4.63	location (Windsor)	13
4.4.63	location (Windsor)	8
5.4.63	Windsor & C & lot	3
8.4.63	location (Windsor)	10
9.4.63	location (Windsor)	11
10.4.63	C	6
11.4.63	C	7
16.4.63	C	4
17.4.63	A & C	4
18.4.63	lot	3
19.4.63	lot	8 (night)
23.4.63	lot & C	8
24.4.63	C	16
25.4.63	location (Windsor)	6
26.4.63	location (Windsor)	11
29.4.63	A	13
30.4.63	location (Windsor)	15
1.5.63	A	7
2.5.63	location & A	12
3.5.63	A	10
6.5.63	A	16
7.5.63	A	24
8.5.63	lot	5

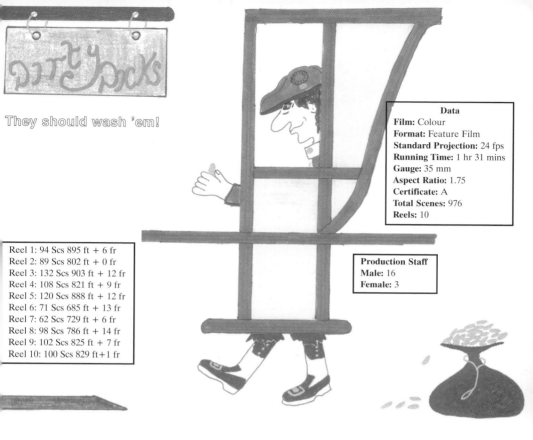

Data
Film: Colour
Format: Feature Film
Standard Projection: 24 fps
Running Time: 1 hr 31 mins
Gauge: 35 mm
Aspect Ratio: 1.75
Certificate: A
Total Scenes: 976
Reels: 10

Reel 1: 94 Scs 895 ft + 6 fr
Reel 2: 89 Scs 802 ft + 0 fr
Reel 3: 132 Scs 903 ft + 12 fr
Reel 4: 108 Scs 821 ft + 9 fr
Reel 5: 120 Scs 888 ft + 12 fr
Reel 6: 71 Scs 685 ft + 13 fr
Reel 7: 62 Scs 729 ft + 6 fr
Reel 8: 98 Scs 786 ft + 14 fr
Reel 9: 102 Scs 825 ft + 7 fr
Reel 10: 100 Scs 829 ft+1 fr

Production Staff
Male: 16
Female: 3

CARRY ON JACK - 1963

This film is shear pantomime, as Peter Rogers described it. Set on the
good ship *Venus*, it follows the four crew members via Spain and back to
England, recapturing their beloved *Venus* on the way. Juliet Mills made
her only appearance of the series in this film. It reportedly took half a day
to film the opening scene, "Kiss me Hardy". This film saw the
introduction of Bernard Cribbins – being taken to Dirty Dicks where he
was told to wave a gold coin in the air to show his attentions were
honourable.

Main Team Billings
1. Kenneth Williams
2. Charles Hawtrey
3. Jim Dale

Film Started: September 1963
Film Finished: October 1963
Film Released: November 1963
Locations Used: 1

Data
Film: B&W
Format: Feature Film
Standard Projection: 24 fps
Running Time: 1 hr 27 mins
Gauge: 35 mm
Aspect Ratio: 1.75
Certificate: A
Reels: 10

RESTRICTED A
RESEARCH ESTABLISHMENT
POSITIVELY NO ADMITTANCE
FOR ANY REASON
WHATSOEVER

235 HLC

EXPRESS

STOP

NO ENTRY BEYOND THIS POINT

Production Staff
Male: 17
Female: 4

THESE DOORS KEPT LOCKED AT ALL TIMES

TOP SECRET LABORATORY
PROF STARK
NO SMOKING

CARRY ON SPYING – 1964

This film was to introduce Barbara Windsor into the Carry On series, a spoof of the popular James Bond films of the time. It was the last film to be made in black and white, and the whole film was shot at Pinewood Studios in the heart of Buckinghamshire. The four bumbling agents (which included Charles Hawtrey as Charlie Bind oh, oh, oh) are making their way across Europe and North Africa in pursuit of the formula which Milchmann (Victor Maddern) had stolen from the laboratory in the opening scene.

Film Started: February 1964
Film Finished: March 1964
Film Released: June 1964
Locations Used: Pinewood

Main Team Billings
1. Kenneth Williams
2. Barbara Windsor
3. Charles Hawtrey
4. Jim Dale

114

MARCUS ET SPENCIUS

I get the point!

Data
Film: Colour
Format: Feature Film
Standard Projection: 24 fps
Running Time: 1 hr 32 mins
Gauge: 35 mm
Aspect Ratio: 1.75
Certificate: A
Reels: 10

Film Started: July 1964
Film Finished: August 1964
Film Released: November 1964
Locations Used: 1

CARRY ON CLEO – 1964

"Friends, Romans, Countrymen, I Know", words uttered by Kenneth Williams as Julius Casesar throughout the film. Made just after the Burton and Taylor film *Cleopatra*, Peter Rogers actually used some of the same set before it was dismantled – cutting down the cost and again another film was produced within budget. Amanda Barrie of *Coronation Street* fame starred in her second and final Carry On, along with Sid James in his fifth film of the series. An excellent performance by Charles Hawtrey as Seneca.

Main Team Billings
1. Sid James
2. Kenneth Williams
3. Charles Hawtrey
4. Kenneth Connor
5. Joan Sims
6. Jim Dale

115

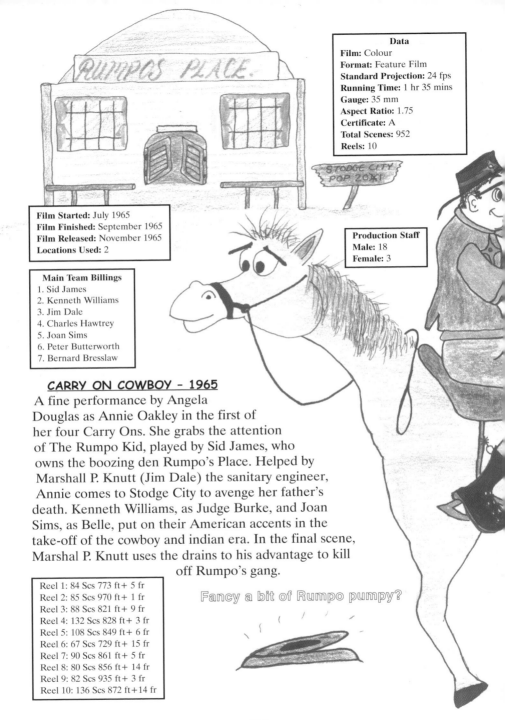

Data
Film: Colour
Format: Feature Film
Standard Projection: 24 fps
Running Time: 1 hr 35 mins
Gauge: 35 mm
Aspect Ratio: 1.75
Certificate: A
Total Scenes: 952
Reels: 10

Film Started: July 1965
Film Finished: September 1965
Film Released: November 1965
Locations Used: 2

Production Staff
Male: 18
Female: 3

Main Team Billings
1. Sid James
2. Kenneth Williams
3. Jim Dale
4. Charles Hawtrey
5. Joan Sims
6. Peter Butterworth
7. Bernard Bresslaw

CARRY ON COWBOY - 1965

A fine performance by Angela
Douglas as Annie Oakley in the first of
her four Carry Ons. She grabs the attention
of The Rumpo Kid, played by Sid James, who
owns the boozing den Rumpo's Place. Helped by
Marshall P. Knutt (Jim Dale) the sanitary engineer,
Annie comes to Stodge City to avenge her father's
death. Kenneth Williams, as Judge Burke, and Joan
Sims, as Belle, put on their American accents in the
take-off of the cowboy and indian era. In the final scene,
Marshal P. Knutt uses the drains to his advantage to kill
off Rumpo's gang.

Reel 1: 84 Scs 773 ft+ 5 fr
Reel 2: 85 Scs 970 ft+ 1 fr
Reel 3: 88 Scs 821 ft+ 9 fr
Reel 4: 132 Scs 828 ft+ 3 fr
Reel 5: 108 Scs 849 ft+ 6 fr
Reel 6: 67 Scs 729 ft+ 15 fr
Reel 7: 90 Scs 861 ft+ 5 fr
Reel 8: 80 Scs 856 ft+ 14 fr
Reel 9: 82 Scs 935 ft+ 3 fr
Reel 10: 136 Scs 872 ft+14 fr

Fancy a bit of Rumpo pumpy?

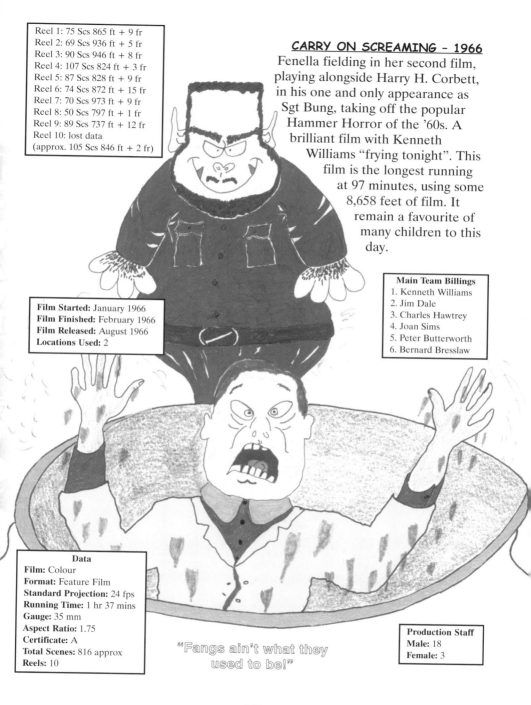

Reel 1: 75 Scs 865 ft + 9 fr
Reel 2: 69 Scs 936 ft + 5 fr
Reel 3: 90 Scs 946 ft + 8 fr
Reel 4: 107 Scs 824 ft + 3 fr
Reel 5: 87 Scs 828 ft + 9 fr
Reel 6: 74 Scs 872 ft + 15 fr
Reel 7: 70 Scs 973 ft + 9 fr
Reel 8: 50 Scs 797 ft + 1 fr
Reel 9: 89 Scs 737 ft + 12 fr
Reel 10: lost data
(approx. 105 Scs 846 ft + 2 fr)

CARRY ON SCREAMING - 1966

Fenella fielding in her second film, playing alongside Harry H. Corbett, in his one and only appearance as Sgt Bung, taking off the popular Hammer Horror of the '60s. A brilliant film with Kenneth Williams "frying tonight". This film is the longest running at 97 minutes, using some 8,658 feet of film. It remain a favourite of many children to this day.

Main Team Billings
1. Kenneth Williams
2. Jim Dale
3. Charles Hawtrey
4. Joan Sims
5. Peter Butterworth
6. Bernard Bresslaw

Film Started: January 1966
Film Finished: February 1966
Film Released: August 1966
Locations Used: 2

Data
Film: Colour
Format: Feature Film
Standard Projection: 24 fps
Running Time: 1 hr 37 mins
Gauge: 35 mm
Aspect Ratio: 1.75
Certificate: A
Total Scenes: 816 approx
Reels: 10

"Fangs ain't what they used to be!"

Production Staff
Male: 18
Female: 3

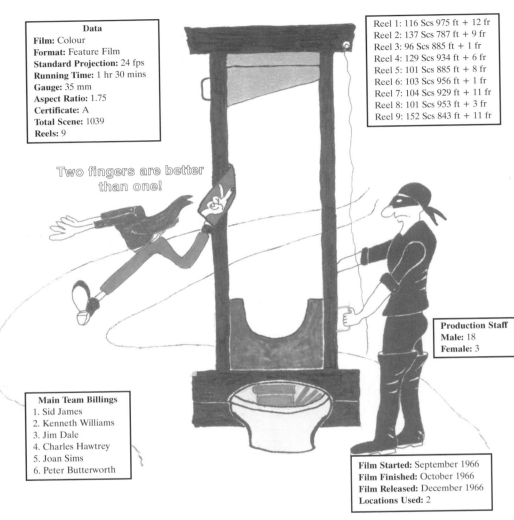

Data
Film: Colour
Format: Feature Film
Standard Projection: 24 fps
Running Time: 1 hr 30 mins
Gauge: 35 mm
Aspect Ratio: 1.75
Certificate: A
Total Scene: 1039
Reels: 9

Reel 1: 116 Scs 975 ft + 12 fr
Reel 2: 137 Scs 787 ft + 9 fr
Reel 3: 96 Scs 885 ft + 1 fr
Reel 4: 129 Scs 934 ft + 6 fr
Reel 5: 101 Scs 885 ft + 8 fr
Reel 6: 103 Scs 956 ft + 1 fr
Reel 7: 104 Scs 929 ft + 11 fr
Reel 8: 101 Scs 953 ft + 3 fr
Reel 9: 152 Scs 843 ft + 11 fr

Two fingers are better than one!

Production Staff
Male: 18
Female: 3

Main Team Billings
1. Sid James
2. Kenneth Williams
3. Jim Dale
4. Charles Hawtrey
5. Joan Sims
6. Peter Butterworth

Film Started: September 1966
Film Finished: October 1966
Film Released: December 1966
Locations Used: 2

CARRY ON DON'T LOSE YOUR HEAD – 1966

Some of the location shots for this film were shot at Waddesdon Manor about six miles from Aylesbury in Buckinghamshire. Based around the French revolution involving the aristocrats and royalists, excellent performances from Williams as Citizen Camembert who's watchword was "every five minutes a sliced loaf", James as The Black Fingernail who left his mark, Dale as Lord Darcy and Butterworth as Citizen Bidet. This was the thirteenth film in the series and certainly not unlucky for some!

CARRY ON FOLLOW THAT CAMEL - 1967

Follow That Camel was the second film under the Rank Organisation banner and the 14th in the series. It saw the introduction of American actor Phil Silvers, famous for his Sgt Bilko. He was reportedly paid £30,000 for his role as Sgt Ernie Nocker, equalling the fee paid to Elke Sommer for *Behind* (1975), making them the highest-paid actors in the series, though Phil never appeared in another Carry On. The location scenes were filmed in the sand dunes at Camber Sands and Rye, Sussex, where the team spent three weeks filming.

Data
Film: Colour
Format: Feature Film
Standard Projection: 24 fps
Running Time: 1 hr 35 mins
Gauge: 35 mm
Aspect Ratio: 1.75
Certificate: A
Total Scenes Used: 216
Reels: 10

Main Team Billings
1. Jim Dale
2. Peter Butterworth
3. Kenneth Williams
4. Charles Hawtrey
5. Joan Sims
6. Bernard Bresslaw

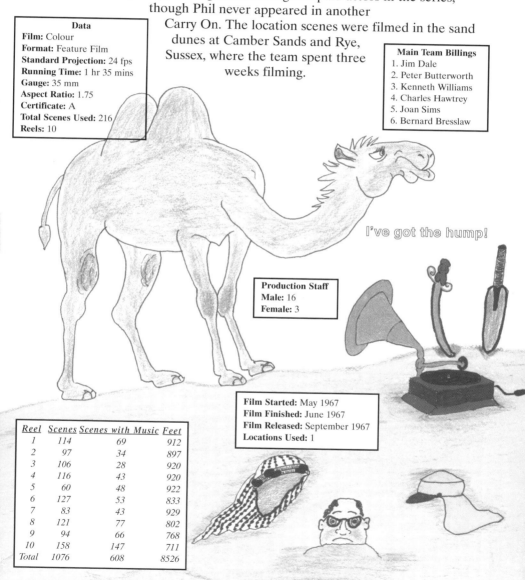

I've got the hump!

Production Staff
Male: 16
Female: 3

Film Started: May 1967
Film Finished: June 1967
Film Released: September 1967
Locations Used: 1

Reel	Scenes	Scenes with Music	Feet
1	114	69	912
2	97	34	897
3	106	28	920
4	116	43	920
5	60	48	922
6	127	53	833
7	83	43	929
8	121	77	802
9	94	66	768
10	158	147	711
Total	1076	608	8526

Carry on Follow That Camel (1967)

Listed below is a breakdown of where and how many scenes were shot.

Date	Pinewood Stage	Number of scenes
2.5.67	location (Camber Sands)	4
3.5.67	location (Camber Sands)	11
4.5.67	location (Icklesham)	4
5.5.67	location (Camber Sands)	5
6.5.67	location (Camber Sands)	11
7.5.67	location (Camber Sands)	9
8.5.67	location (Camber Sands)	16
9.5.67	location (Camber Sands)	7
10.5.67	location (Camber Sands)	13
11.5.67	location (Camber Sands)	6
12.5.67	location (Camber Sands)	6
13.5.67	location (Camber Sands)	2
15.5.67	location (Camber Sands)	5
16.5.67	location (Camber Sands)	10
17.5.67	location (Camber Sands)	7
19.5.67	H	4
22.5.67 (strike over)	H & F	11
23.5.67 (rain delay)	lot	5
24.5.67 (rain delay)	lot	3
25.5.67 (rain delay)	lot	6
26.5.67	H	4
30.5.67	F	5
31.5.67	H & lot	7
1.6.67 (Bad light)	lot	2
2.6.67	lot	9
5.6.67	lot	9
6.6.67	lot	11
7.6.67	F	3
8.6.67	F&H	3
9.6.67	H&F	4
12.6.67	F	4
13.6.67	F	5
14.6.67	location (Swankleys)	2
15.6.67	location & F	4
16.6.67	F	4
19.6.67	location (Osterley Park)	3
20.6.67	F & H	7
21.6.67	H	3
22.6.67	H & F	6
23.6.67	lot & H	11

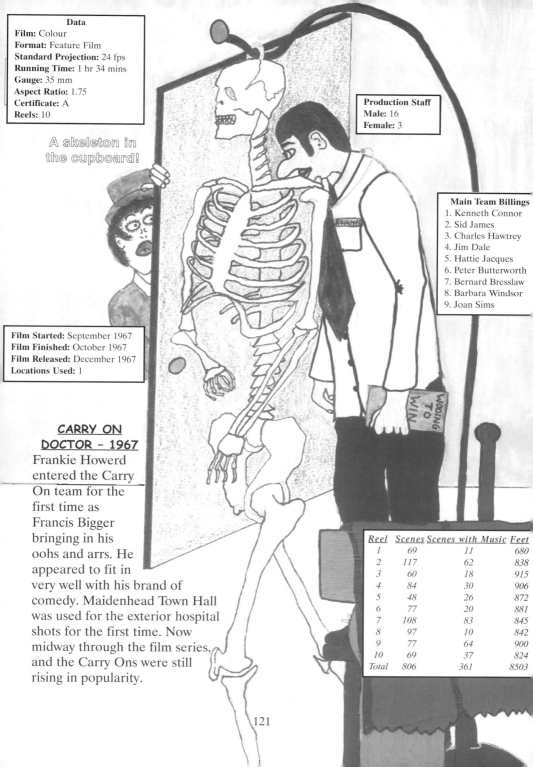

Data
Film: Colour
Format: Feature Film
Standard Projection: 24 fps
Running Time: 1 hr 34 mins
Gauge: 35 mm
Aspect Ratio: 1.75
Certificate: A
Reels: 10

A skeleton in the cupboard!

Production Staff
Male: 16
Female: 3

Main Team Billings
1. Kenneth Connor
2. Sid James
3. Charles Hawtrey
4. Jim Dale
5. Hattie Jacques
6. Peter Butterworth
7. Bernard Bresslaw
8. Barbara Windsor
9. Joan Sims

Film Started: September 1967
Film Finished: October 1967
Film Released: December 1967
Locations Used: 1

CARRY ON DOCTOR – 1967

Frankie Howerd entered the Carry On team for the first time as Francis Bigger bringing in his oohs and arrs. He appeared to fit in very well with his brand of comedy. Maidenhead Town Hall was used for the exterior hospital shots for the first time. Now midway through the film series, and the Carry Ons were still rising in popularity.

Reel	Scenes	Scenes with Music	Feet
1	69	11	680
2	117	62	838
3	60	18	915
4	84	30	906
5	48	26	872
6	77	20	881
7	108	83	845
8	97	10	842
9	77	64	900
10	69	37	824
Total	806	361	8503

CARRY ON UP THE KHYBER - 1968

This film, along with *Cleo*, appeared in the top 100 British films ever made. One of the costume greats of the series, it was the only time the team ventured out of England, to Snowdonia, North Wales, to film the "Khyber Pass". It was obviously an excellent location choice as an old friend of Peter Rogers phoned him after seeing the film to say he recognised the area as a part of India he had stayed in while serving in the army.

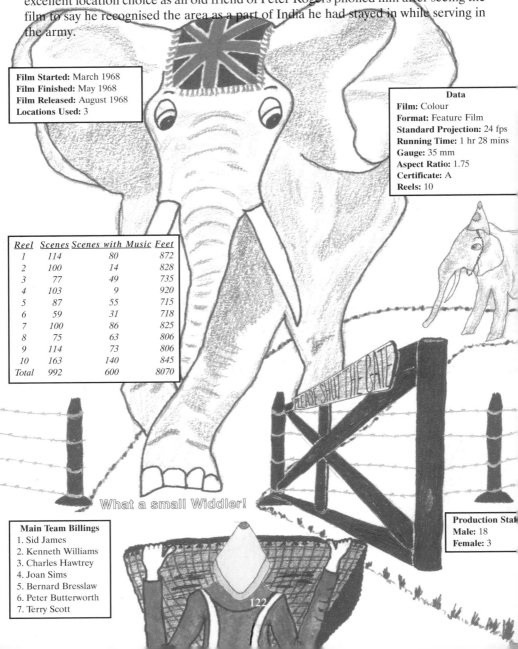

Film Started: March 1968
Film Finished: May 1968
Film Released: August 1968
Locations Used: 3

Data
Film: Colour
Format: Feature Film
Standard Projection: 24 fps
Running Time: 1 hr 28 mins
Gauge: 35 mm
Aspect Ratio: 1.75
Certificate: A
Reels: 10

Reel	Scenes	Scenes with Music	Feet
1	114	80	872
2	100	14	828
3	77	49	735
4	103	9	920
5	87	55	715
6	59	31	718
7	100	86	825
8	75	63	806
9	114	73	806
10	163	140	845
Total	992	600	8070

PLEASE SHUT THE GATE

What a small Widdler!

Main Team Billings
1. Sid James
2. Kenneth Williams
3. Charles Hawtrey
4. Joan Sims
5. Bernard Bresslaw
6. Peter Butterworth
7. Terry Scott

Production Staff
Male: 18
Female: 3

CARRY ON CAMPING – 1968

Made midway through the comedy series, this film, along with *Screaming* (1966) and *Up The Khyber* (1968) is one of the people's favourites. Set in the Paradise Campsite it brings out all the fun of outdoor life. The filming took place in October/November and was made to look like summer by spraying the grass with green paint. *Camping* is one of the funniest with the jokes coming thick and fast, undoubtedly one of the Rothwell's finest.

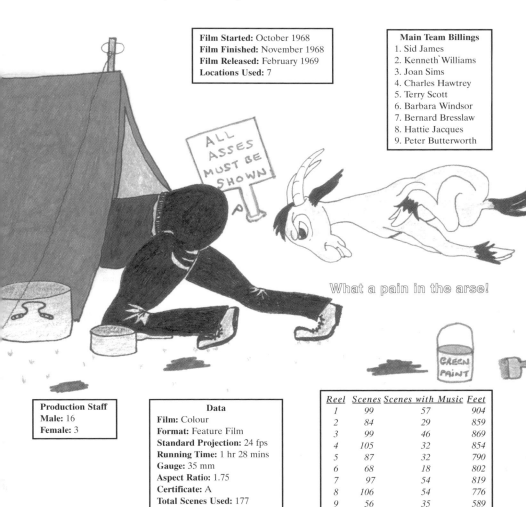

Film Started: October 1968
Film Finished: November 1968
Film Released: February 1969
Locations Used: 7

Main Team Billings
1. Sid James
2. Kenneth Williams
3. Joan Sims
4. Charles Hawtrey
5. Terry Scott
6. Barbara Windsor
7. Bernard Bresslaw
8. Hattie Jacques
9. Peter Butterworth

Production Staff
Male: 16
Female: 3

Data
Film: Colour
Format: Feature Film
Standard Projection: 24 fps
Running Time: 1 hr 28 mins
Gauge: 35 mm
Aspect Ratio: 1.75
Certificate: A
Total Scenes Used: 177
Reels: 10

Reel	Scenes	Scenes with Music	Feet
1	99	57	904
2	84	29	859
3	99	46	869
4	105	32	854
5	87	32	790
6	68	18	802
7	97	54	819
8	106	54	776
9	56	35	589
10	106	72	750
Total	907	429	8012

Carry on Camping (1968)

A breakdown of where and how many scenes were shot for many peoples' favourite film.

Date	Pinewood Stage	Number of scenes
7.10.68	lot (orchard)	4
8.10.68	north tunnel	7
9.10.68	lot	7
10.10.68	lot	5
11.10.68	lot & north tunnel	8
14.10.68	lot	4
15.10.68	lot	7
16.10.68	lot & north tunnel	7
17.10.68	lot	9
18.10.68	north tunnel	5
21.10.68	lot	9
22.10.68	lot	8
23.10.68	C	9
24.10.68	lot & C	12
25.10.68	lot & C	9
28.10.68	C	5
29.10.68	club house & gardens	4
30.10.68	C & location (Northolt)	2
31.10.68	C & location (Northolt)	2
1.11.68	C & location (Northolt)	3
4.11.68	location	6
5.11.68	lot	3
6.11.68	lot	4
7.11.68	C	5
8.11.68	C	8
11.11.68	C	3
12.11.68	location	7
13.11.68	location	5
14.11.68	location & lot	8
15.11.68	location	4
18.11.68	C	9
19.11.68	C	1 (night)
20.11.68	C & Pinewood cul-de-sac	3
21.11.68	A	8
22.11.68	A	1

No waiting time on this trolley!

Film Started: March 1969
Film Finished: May 1969
Film Released: August 1969
Locations Used: 3

CARRY ON AGAIN DOCTOR - 1969

The eighteenth film of the series and the introduction of Patsy Rowlands into the Carry On team. Jim Dale as Dr Nookey who struck gold when he came across Gladstone Screwer (Sid James) on the Beatific Islands, Nookey came back with a weight-reducing serum and went into partnership with Ellen Moore (Joan Sims) to form the Moore-Nookey clinic. Jim Dale actually did his own stunts. In the scene where he was on the hospital trolley going down the stairs he ended up in a real hospital, breaking a bone in his arm.

Main Team Billings
1. Sid James
2. Jim Dale
3. Kenneth Williams
4. Charles Hawtrey
5. Joan Sims
6. Barbara Windsor
7. Hattie Jacques
8. Patsy Rowlands
9. Peter Butterworth

Data
Film: Colour
Format: Feature Film
Standard Projection: 24 fps
Running Time: 1 hr 29 mins
Gauge: 35 mm
Aspect Ratio: 1.75
Certificate: A
Reels: 10

Reel	Scenes	Scenes with Music	Feet
1	86	30	907
2	90	32	793
3	91	71	738
4	97	94	808
5	95	40	889
6	70	33	804
7	74	37	812
8	83	10	734
9	83	28	814
10	99	44	745
Total	868	419	8044

Production Staff
Male: 15
Female: 3

125

Data
Film: Colour
Format: Feature Film
Standard Projection: 24 fps
Running Time: 1 hr 29 mins
Gauge: 35 mm
Aspect Ratio: 1.75
Certificate: A
Reels: 10

Film Started: October 1969
Film Finished: November 1969
Film Released: March 1970
Locations Used: 2

Main Team Billings
1. Sid James
2. Charles Hawtrey
3. Joan Sims
4. Kenneth Connor
5. Bernard Bresslaw
6. Terry Scott

Reel	Scenes	Scenes with Music	Feet
1	94	45	823
2	87	13	712
3	117	69	829
4	100	57	901
5	52	25	753
6	91	68	885
7	140	90	834
8	134	68	899
9	93	51	749
10	140	71	812
Total	1048	557	8197

One for the pot!

DANGER CONCEALED TREE

Production Staff
Male: 15
Female: 3

CARRY ON UP THE JUNGLE - 1969

This film was Frankie Howerd's second and final Carry On. Almost entirely filmed at Pinewood Studios with the use of wildlife footage, this was not the king of the jungle for most fans. This film was one of only five that Kenneth Williams did not appear in.

Reel	Scenes	Scenes with Music	Feet
1	118	74	892
2	87	29	813
3	113	103	890
4	126	118	801
5	82	10	839
6	123	68	902
7	107	15	835
8	90	4	758
9	110	72	778
10	88	57	623
Total	1044	488	8131

Main Team Billings
1. Sid James
2. Kenneth Williams
3. Charles Hawtrey
4. Hattie Jacques
5. Joan Sims
6. Bernard Bresslaw
7. Terry Scott
8. Patsy Rowlands
9. Peter Butterworth

CARRY ON LOVING – 1970

Now two-thirds of the way through the series, *Loving* was filmed on location in Park Street, Windsor where the Wedded Bliss agency was situated, run by Sid and Hattie. The final scene brings out the good old slap-stick custard pie in the face – and real cream was used. "It took three days to shoot this scene and as everything had to be left ready for the next day the stench was terrible," Patsy Rowlands said when interviewed at a Carry On convention.

Data
Film: Colour
Format: Feature Film
Standard Projection: 24 fps
Running Time: 1 hr 28 mins
Gauge: 35 mm
Aspect Ratio: 1.75
Certificate: A
Total Scenes Used: 262
Reels: 10

Sidney Bliss outside Esme's door pouring water all over himself to prove to Esme that he couldn't go through life without her.

Production Staff
Male: 17
Female: 3

Film Started: April 1970
Film Finished: May 1970
Film Released: September 1970
Locations Used: 6

Too hot to handle!

CARRY ON HENRY - 1970

One of the all-time historical greats of the series, where Henry was renowned for chasing the women with his chopper. Sid James' famous phrase "Inn it again" was used when he fell into a pile of manure after being chased by the wenches' father, played by Derek Francis. It was on the set of *Henry* that screenwriter Talbot Rothwell was caught with the big red book for *This Is Your Life*.

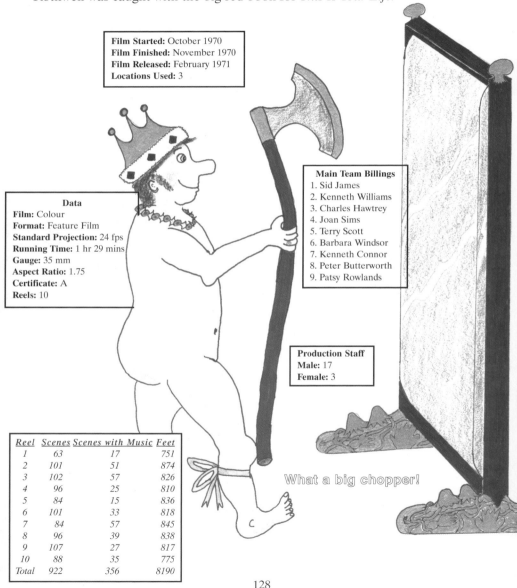

Film Started: October 1970
Film Finished: November 1970
Film Released: February 1971
Locations Used: 3

Data
Film: Colour
Format: Feature Film
Standard Projection: 24 fps
Running Time: 1 hr 29 mins
Gauge: 35 mm
Aspect Ratio: 1.75
Certificate: A
Reels: 10

Main Team Billings
1. Sid James
2. Kenneth Williams
3. Charles Hawtrey
4. Joan Sims
5. Terry Scott
6. Barbara Windsor
7. Kenneth Connor
8. Peter Butterworth
9. Patsy Rowlands

Production Staff
Male: 17
Female: 3

What a big chopper!

Reel	Scenes	Scenes with Music	Feet
1	63	17	751
2	101	51	874
3	102	57	826
4	96	25	810
5	84	15	836
6	101	33	818
7	84	57	845
8	96	39	838
9	107	27	817
10	88	35	775
Total	922	356	8190

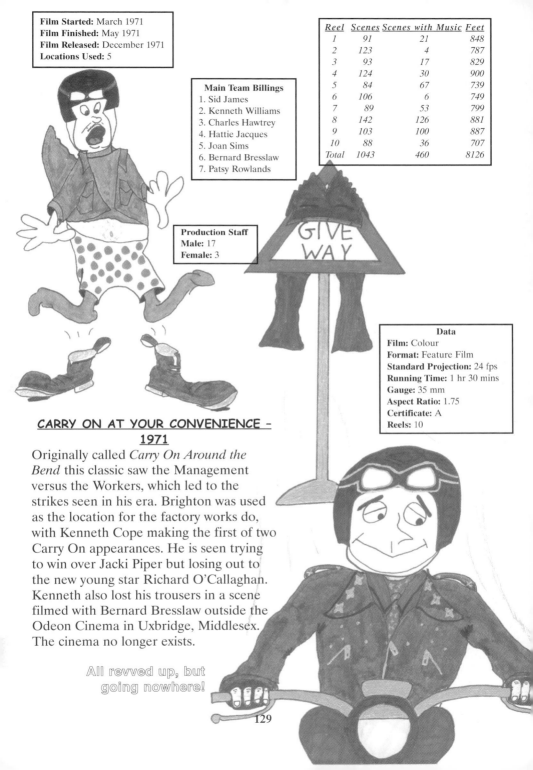

Film Started: March 1971
Film Finished: May 1971
Film Released: December 1971
Locations Used: 5

Reel	Scenes	Scenes with Music	Feet
1	91	21	848
2	123	4	787
3	93	17	829
4	124	30	900
5	84	67	739
6	106	6	749
7	89	53	799
8	142	126	881
9	103	100	887
10	88	36	707
Total	1043	460	8126

Main Team Billings
1. Sid James
2. Kenneth Williams
3. Charles Hawtrey
4. Hattie Jacques
5. Joan Sims
6. Bernard Bresslaw
7. Patsy Rowlands

Production Staff
Male: 17
Female: 3

Data
Film: Colour
Format: Feature Film
Standard Projection: 24 fps
Running Time: 1 hr 30 mins
Gauge: 35 mm
Aspect Ratio: 1.75
Certificate: A
Reels: 10

CARRY ON AT YOUR CONVENIENCE – 1971

Originally called *Carry On Around the Bend* this classic saw the Management versus the Workers, which led to the strikes seen in his era. Brighton was used as the location for the factory works do, with Kenneth Cope making the first of two Carry On appearances. He is seen trying to win over Jacki Piper but losing out to the new young star Richard O'Callaghan. Kenneth also lost his trousers in a scene filmed with Bernard Bresslaw outside the Odeon Cinema in Uxbridge, Middlesex. The cinema no longer exists.

All revved up, but going nowhere!

Data

Film: Colour
Format: Feature Film
Standard Projection: 24 fps
Running Time: 1 hr 27 mins
Gauge: 35 mm
Aspect Ratio: 1.75
Certificate: A
Total Scenes Used: 157
Reels: 10

Production Staff

Male: 17
Female: 4

Reel	Scenes	Scenes with Music	Feet
1	83	37	825
2	91	40	793
3	110	31	827
4	133	71	838
5	91	33	891
6	89	22	704
7	98	50	876
8	97	53	766
9	93	61	840
10	111	74	706
Total	996	472	8066

CARRY ON MATRON – 1971

The last of the medical Carry Ons. *Matron*, the 23rd film of the series, brings out an excellent performance from Kenneth Williams as the hypochondriac Sir Bernard Cutting – the overall top team member in number of films appeared in. Sid James and Bill Maynard dress in disguise to locate the whereabouts of the pills stored at Finisham Maternity Hospital. This film saw the departure of Jacki Piper after her two-year contact ended. Mostly filmed on location in Ascot and Denham village close to Pinewood Studios – an early seventies film in the middle of an outstanding era of the Carry Ons.

Film Started: October 1971
Film Finished: November 1971
Film Released: May 1972
Locations Used: 3

Main Team Billings

1. Sid James
2. Kenneth Williams
3. Charles Hawtrey
4. Hattie Jacques
5. Joan Sims
6. Bernard Bresslaw
7. Barbara Windsor
8 Kenneth Connor
9. Terry Scott
10. Patsy Rowlands
11. Jack Douglas

130

Carry On Matron 1971

Listed below is a breakdown of where and how many scenes were shot for this, the last medical comedy of the series.

Date	Pinewood Stage	Number of scenes
11.10.71	B	7
12.10.71	B	4
13.10.71	B	5
14.10.71	B&A	6
18.10.71	A	7
20.10.71	A	10
21.10.71	A	4
22.10.71	A&B	4
25.10.71	B	5
26.10.71	location (Ascot)	19
27.10.71	location (Ascot)	13
28.10.71	B	4
29.10.71	B	10
1.11.71	B	2
2.11.71	B & location (Denham)	11
3.11.71	B	8
4.11.71	A	6
5.11.71	A	8
8.11.71	A	4
9.11.71	A	6
10.11.71	A	10
11.11.71	A	3
12.11.71	A	7
15.11.71	A	3
16.11.71	A	2
17.11.71	A & lot	8
18.11.71	north tunnel	2
23.11.71	theatre 5	1
25.11.71	theatre 5	1
26.11.71	theatre 5	1

Main Team Billings
1. Sid James
2. Kenneth Williams
3. Charles Hawtrey
4. Joan Sims
5 Kenneth Connor
6. Hattie Jacques
7. Bernard Bresslaw
8. Terry Scott
9. Barbara Windsor
10. Patsy Rowlands
11. Jack Douglas

Reel	Scenes	Scenes with Music	Feet
1	87	26	820
2	94	84	777
3	138	45	868
4	112	81	870
5	102	42	827
6	114	74	766
7	101	79	722
8	113	27	732
9	102	65	870
10	103	50	796
Total	1066	573	8048

Production Staff
Male: 17
Female: 2

Film Started: April 1972
Film Finished: May 1972
Film Released: December 1972
Locations Used: 3

That's the biggest hole
I've ever fell into!

Data
Film: Colour
Format: Feature Film
Standard Projection: 24 fps
Running Time: 1 hr 28 mins
Gauge: 35 mm
Aspect Ratio: 1.75
Certificate: A
Total Scenes Used: 262
Reels: 10

CARRY ON ABROAD - 1972

Set in the half-finished Elsbels Palace Hotel in Spain (which, of course, was Pinewood Studios). The Carry On team creates mayhem as the hilarious holiday laughter comes thick and fast. The furthest they travelled to make this film was to Bagshot in Surrey, for the dirt road leading to Elsbels (some holiday destination). Petter Butterworth played the hotel owner and many other charactes. Before the hotel was fully constructed it fell down under the pressure of severe weather conditions.

The Palace hotel

I'll take BUS anytime Ha Ha

Reel	Scenes	Scenes with Music	Feet
1	122	33	878
2	105	22	730
3	108	37	757
4	139	63	790
5	118	22	819
6	114	33	825
7	61	29	724
8	97	45	739
9	115	43	833
10	190	162	880
Total	1169	489	7975

FIRCOMBE SUNSHINE RECORD

BEAUTY QUEENS GO HOME

WOMENS LIB EQUALITY OR BUST

Main Team Billings
1. Sid James
2. Barbara Windsor
3. Joan Sims
4 Kenneth Connor
5. Bernard Bresslaw
6. Peter Butterworth
7. Jack Douglas
8. Patsy Rowlands

Data
Film: Colour
Format: Feature Film
Standard Projection: 24 fps
Running Time: 1 hr 28 mins
Gauge: 35 mm
Aspect Ratio: 1.75
Certificate: A
Total Scenes Used: 131
Reels: 10

CARRY ON GIRLS – 1973

Girls was the 25th film of the series and again, like *At Your Convenience* (1971), the team used Brighton for the location shoot as the fictitious town of Fircombe, where the womens movement launched operation spoilsport against Sidney Fiddler and the contest beauty queens.

Film Started: April 1973
Film Finished: May 1973
Film Released: November 1973
Locations Used: 6

Production Staff
Male: 18
Female: 3

Carry On Girls (1973)

Listed below is a breakdown of where and how many scenes were shot in this the second of the Brighton location films.

Date	Pinewood Stage	Number of scenes
16.4.73	location (Brighton)	2
17.4.73	location (Brighton)	8
18.4.73	location (Brighton)	5
19.4.73	E	3
24.4.73	E	11
25.4.73	E	6
26.4.73	E	1
27.4.73	E	3
30.4.73	E	1
1.5.73	E	2
2.5.73	E	8
3.5.73	E	6
4.5.73	E	20
7.5.73	E	5
8.5.73	E	7
9.5.73	E&C	3
10.5.73	C	12
11.5.73	C	5
14.5.73	E	3
15.5.73	location (Madeira Drive Brighton)	6
16.5.73	location & E	7
17.5.73	location (Slough)	5
18.5.73	E	3
21.5.73	E	7
22.5.73	E	2
23.5.73	E	3
24.5.73	E	3

Pinewood Green cul-de-sac scene used in Camping *(1968), and* Emmannuelle *ten years later in 1978. Note this scene was filmed on 20th November 1968.*

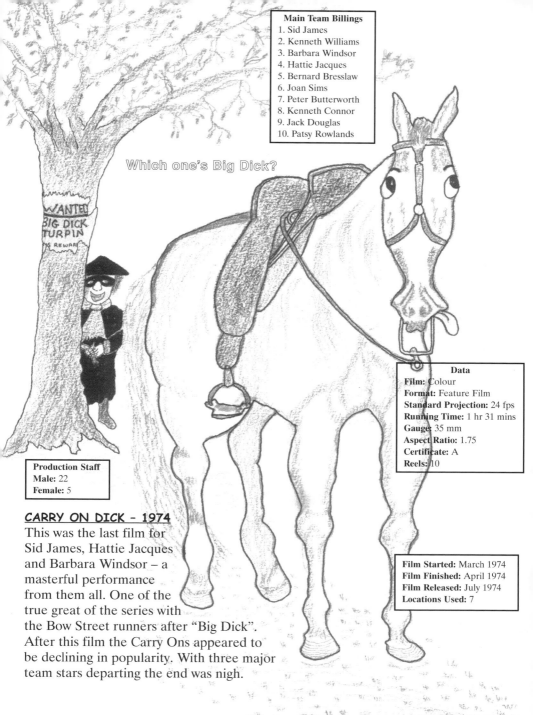

Main Team Billings
1. Sid James
2. Kenneth Williams
3. Barbara Windsor
4. Hattie Jacques
5. Bernard Bresslaw
6. Joan Sims
7. Peter Butterworth
8. Kenneth Connor
9. Jack Douglas
10. Patsy Rowlands

Which one's Big Dick?

WANTED
BIG DICK
TURPIN
£ REWARD

Data
Film: Colour
Format: Feature Film
Standard Projection: 24 fps
Running Time: 1 hr 31 mins
Gauge: 35 mm
Aspect Ratio: 1.75
Certificate: A
Reels: 10

Production Staff
Male: 22
Female: 5

CARRY ON DICK - 1974

This was the last film for Sid James, Hattie Jacques and Barbara Windsor – a masterful performance from them all. One of the true great of the series with the Bow Street runners after "Big Dick". After this film the Carry Ons appeared to be declining in popularity. With three major team stars departing the end was nigh.

Film Started: March 1974
Film Finished: April 1974
Film Released: July 1974
Locations Used: 7

135

Production Staff
Male: 15
Female: 3

Data
Film: Colour
Format: Feature Film
Standard Projection: 24 fps
Running Time: 1 hr 30 mins
Gauge: 35 mm
Aspect Ratio: 1.75
Certificate: A
Reels: 10

Main Team Billi
1. Kenneth Willia
2. Bernard Bressl
3 Kenneth Conno
4. Joan Sims
5. Jack Douglas
6. Peter Butterwo
7. Patsy Rowlands

Film Started: March 1975
Film Finished: April 1975
Film Released: December 1975
Locations Used: 5

Reel	Scenes	Scenes with Music	Feet
1	134	3	828
2	137	25	893
3	122	27	818
4	85	58	744
5	103	22	869
6	82	10	854
7	105	24	729
8	114	19	841
9	104	58	736
10	152	89	882
Total	1138	335	8194

Show us your clickers!

CARRY ON BEHIND - 1975

The last of the great Carry Ons. In this film they returned to the same field where they filmed *Camping* some seven years earlier. Complete with a talking mynah bird uttering naughty words such as "show us your knickers" upsetting the campers. The voice for the bird was none other than Gerald Thomas, drirector of the Carry On films. The scriptwriter for this film was Dave Freeman, taking over from Talbot Rothwell – a tough act to follow but Dave managed it very well.

Main Team Billings
1. Kenneth Connor
2. Jack Douglas
3. Peter Butterworth
4. Joan Sims

Production Staff
Male: 20
Female: 4

Rise and shine – stand to attention!

CARRY ON ENGLAND - 1976

The second time the Carry On team visited the army barracks in their eighteen year run. This film starred Windsor (lovely boy) Davies in his second and last Carry On. The men and women of the camp could not keep their hands off each other and even took to tunnelling into each others' barracks but never succeeding to meet, under the nose of Sgt Major Tiger Bloomer.

Film Started: May 1976
Film Finished: June 1976
Film Released: October 1976
Locations Used: Pinewood

Reel	Scenes	Scenes with Music	Feet
1	107	33	893
2	110	14	909
3	90	21	926
4	90	15	864
5	106	22	855
6	71	15	849
7	100	59	942
8	125	20	920
9	136	34	880
Total	935	233	8038

Data
Film: Colour
Format: Feature Film
Standard Projection: 24 fps
Running Time: 1 hr 29 mins
Gauge: 35 mm
Aspect Ratio: 1.75
Certificate: A
Reels: 9

Main Team Billings
1. Kenneth Williams
2. Kenneth Connor
3. Jack Douglas
4. Joan Sims
5. Peter Butterworth

Hello cheeky!

Production Staff
Male: 20
Female: 4

Data
Film: Colour
Format: Feature Film
Standard Projection: 24 f
Running Time: 1 hr 28 mi
Gauge: 35 mm
Aspect Ratio: 1.75
Certificate: AA
Reels: 10

CARRY ON EMMANNUELLE - 1978

The was film number thirty in a twenty-year span of Carry Ons. By now they had seemed to lose their way. Kenneth Williams played Emile Prevert putting on a French accent which really wasn't him. Suzanne Danielle starred in her only Carry On as the sex-starved wife of Emile, she even tried to chat up the palace guards! Some of the team were present, but with the exception of *Columbus* fourteen years later, the series was as good as finished. What a shame!

Film Started: April 1978
Film Finished: May 1978
Film Released: November 1978
Locations Used: 4

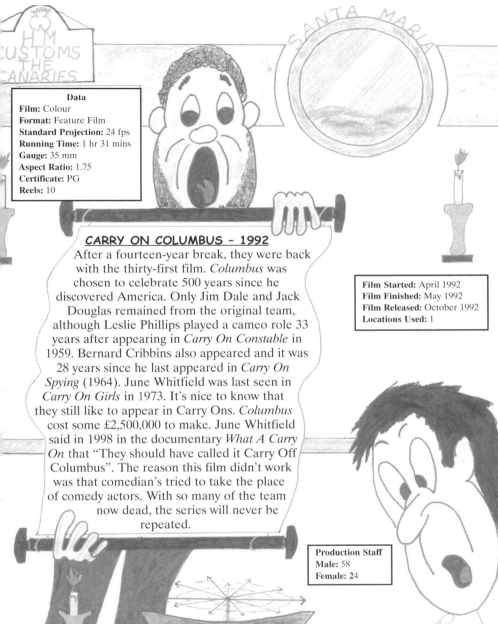

Data
Film: Colour
Format: Feature Film
Standard Projection: 24 fps
Running Time: 1 hr 31 mins
Gauge: 35 mm
Aspect Ratio: 1.75
Certificate: PG
Reels: 10

CARRY ON COLUMBUS – 1992

After a fourteen-year break, they were back with the thirty-first film. *Columbus* was chosen to celebrate 500 years since he discovered America. Only Jim Dale and Jack Douglas remained from the original team, although Leslie Phillips played a cameo role 33 years after appearing in *Carry On Constable* in 1959. Bernard Cribbins also appeared and it was 28 years since he last appeared in *Carry On Spying* (1964). June Whitfield was last seen in *Carry On Girls* in 1973. It's nice to know that they still like to appear in Carry Ons. *Columbus* cost some £2,500,000 to make. June Whitfield said in 1998 in the documentary *What A Carry On* that "They should have called it Carry Off Columbus". The reason this film didn't work was that comedian's tried to take the place of comedy actors. With so many of the team now dead, the series will never be repeated.

Film Started: April 1992
Film Finished: May 1992
Film Released: October 1992
Locations Used: 1

Production Staff
Male: 58
Female: 24

Main Team Billings
1. Jim Dale
2. Jack Douglas

All in a spin! – never to be again!

Appendix 1
Carry On Books & Related Books

On The Way I Lost It, Frankie Howerd (W H Allen 1976)
The Carry On Book, Kenneth Eastaugh (David & Charles 1978)
Just Williams – An Autobiography, Kenneth Williams (J M Dent 1985)
What A Carry On – The Offical Story of the Carry On Film Series, Sally & Nina Hibbin (Hamlyn 1988)
Kenneth Williams, Michael Freedland (Weidenfeld 1990)
Barbara – The Laughter and Tears Of a Cockney Sparrow, Barbara Windsor (Century 1990)
Titter Ye Not! – The Life of Frankie Howerd, William Hall (Grafton 1992)
The Kenneth Williams Diaries, Russell Davies (Harper Collins 1993)
The Kenneth Williams Letters, Russell Davies (Harper Collins 1994)
Sid James, Cliff Goodwin (Century 1994)
The Carry On Quiz Book, Graham C Bromwich (Laid Back 1996)
Carry On Laughing – A Celebration, Adrian Rigelsford (Virgin 1996)
The Carry On Companion, Robert Ross (Batsford 1996 & 1998)
The Carry On Again & Quiz Book, Graham C Bromwich (Laid Back 1998)
Carry On Uncensored, Morris Bright & Robert Ross (Boxtree 1999)
High Spirits, Joan Sims (2000)
Frankie Howerd – The Illustrated Biography, Mick Middles (Headline 2000)
The Life and Works of Peter Rogers, Morris Bright & Robert Ross (BBC 2000)
All Of Me – My Extraordinary Life, Barbara Windsor (Headline 2000)
The Lost Carry Ons, Morris Bright & Robert Ross (Virgin 2000)
And June Whitfield, June Whitfield (Bantam 2000)
The Complete Sid James, Robert Ross (Reynolds & Hearn Ltd 2000)
The Complete Frankie Howerd, Robert Ross (Reynolds & Hearn Ltd 2001)
Charles Hawtrey, "The Man who was Private Widdle", Roger Lewis (Faber & Faber 2001)
A Twitch in Time Jack Douglas' Life Story, Sue Benwell (Able 2002)
Carry On Films, Mark Campbell (Pocket Essentials 2002)

Appendix 2
Carry On Clubs & Societies

The British Comedy Appreciation Society
"Laughter Lines", 1A Woodbury, Castle Road, Woking, Surrey GU21 4ET

Cor! – The British Comedy Magazine
24 Richmond Road, Basingstoke, Hampshire RG21 5NX

The Hattie Jacques Appreciation Society
34 Freemantle Avenue, Sutton Trust Estate, Hull HU9 4RH

The Kenneth Williams & Sid James Society (Founded 1988)
"Stop Messin' About!", 27 Brookmead Way, Orpington, Kent BR5 2BQ

The Grand Order of Newts Carry On Fanzine Magazine
23 Braithwaite Drive, Colchester, Essex, CO4 5XG

The Official Carry On Fan Club (Founded 1993)
3 Littleburn Close, Houghton-Le-Spring, Tyne & Wear, DH4 5HJ

Jack Douglas Headquarters
RWCC, PO Box 19, Ventnor, PO38 1WD

The British Comedy Society
28 Clarendon Road, Boreham Wood, Hertfordshire WD6 1BJ

Carry On – Line Internet Site
51 Hudson Road, Bexley Heath, Kent DA7 4PQ www.carryonline.com

Carry On Fan Club (Founded 1996)
43 Hunters Drive, Seaton, Workington, Cumbria CA14 1RN

"Inn it Again"
The Sid James Magazine, Svarttlonnheia 75, 4645 Nodeland, Norway

Appendix 3
Carry On Merchandise

Classic Memorabilia is possibly the largest retailer of Carry On merchandise in the country. Their merchandise includes videos, DVDs, audio cassettes, books, memorabilia, autographs and much, much more. For Carry On and many other classic comedies, please visit the Classic Memorabilia website:

www.classic-memorabilia.co.uk

or send for further information to the address below:

Classic Memorabilia
25 Arundel Crescent
Solihull
West Midlands
B92 8RQ

Email: sales@classic-memorabilia.co.uk

The triangle on Pinewood Green Estate.
Scene used in Carry On Cabby *(1963)*

Appendix 4
An Example of a Daily Progress Report
In the production of a Carry On Film

Number: _____

Production: _____

Production Number: _____ Day: _____ Date: _____

Set(s): _____ Days on Set: _____ Stage: _____

Director: _____ Cameraman: _____

Picture commenced: _____

Unit call: _____ finished: _____   Camera schedule days _____
Camera days to date _____

	Studio	Location

	Footage				Screen Time		
	Picture		Sound		Studio		Location
	Gross	Print	Gross	Print	mins	secs	mins	secs
Today								
Previous								
To date								

Colour – Stills

Produce	ref	published

Scenes

Total in script:	
Shot to date:	
Scene shot today:	
Schedule for tomorrow:	
Scene number tomorrow:	

Artistes

Contract	Daily Rate

Special Equipment:
Vehicle/Animals:
Remarks:

About the Author

Kevin Snelgrove was born on 15th February 1960 in Frome, a small town in the countryside of East Somerset. He has been a fan of the Carry Ons since he was nine years of age, and is now considered one of the countries leading experts.

He has attended many Carry On events held at Pinewood Studios where he has made brief appearances on television, video and DVD, he has also featured in audio productions with Peter Rogers and Jack Douglas.

In March 2000 he attended the BBC's *The Hall of Fame* with Barbara Windsor. In October of the same year a selection of his work from the book was published in *The Grand Order of Newts,* a Carry On fanzine magazine. He has also worked as a consultant for production companies making Carry On programmes for television.

So lets Carry On for years to come and hope it never stops!

Carry On Producer Peter Rogers with author Kevin Snelgrove
Taken at Pinewood Studios, 5th November 2000